php|architect's Guide to Date and Time Programming

by Derick Rethans

php|architect
nanobooks

php|architect's Guide to Date and Time Programming

First Edition: February 2009
ISBN: **978-0-9738621-5-7**
Produced in Canada
Printed in the United States

Disclaimer

Written by	Derick Rethans
Published by	Marco Tabini & Associates, Inc.
	28 Bombay Ave.
	Toronto, ON M3H 1B7
	Canada
	(416) 630-6202 / (877) 630-6202
	info@phparch.com / www.phparch.com
Publisher	Marco Tabini
Technical Reviewers	Scott MacVicar and Ole Marius Smestad
Layout and Design	Arbi Arzoumani
Managing Editor	Elizabeth Naramore
Finance and Resource Management	Emanuela Corso

Contents

Acknowledgments

This book wouldn't be what it is without the help of many. First of all I would like to thank my technical reviewers Scott MacVicar and Ole Marius Smestad for their time and many useful comments.

I would also like to thank my editor Elizabeth Naramore for her support and guidance while working on the book.

Chapter 1

Introduction

"There is no time like the present"—an old proverb hitting the nail exactly on the head. However, it is not so simple to actually represent the present time. Over the past centuries humankind went from using sundials to determine what time of day it was, to highly advanced atomic clocks. Besides those advances in technology, there are other elements that greatly increase the difficulty of answering the question "What time is it?". This book is all about handling "time" with PHP, but that can not be correctly done without a basic introduction on how all the different aspects fit into place.

A Little History

People have been known to track time as far back as 5000 years ago. The old civilizations used sundials to determine the current time. The time that their sundials would display depended on where the Sun was at a specific moment. Because the Earth is not in a circular orbit around the Sun, the time that was obtained from the sundials could differ with a maximum of 15 minutes from *true solar time*. Over the course of history, the true solar time was not accurate enough anymore, and the *mean solar time* was created to account for the differences caused by the Earth's orbit. The *mean solar time* is basically an average of when then Sun would be due south. The length of a *mean solar day* is about 86400 seconds, although this is increasing slightly as time moves forward. However, the mean solar time is only valid for one specific location on Earth. In other words, the mean solar time is actually a *local mean time*. This was often not an issue in the early 19th century, when mechanical clocks and sundials were accurate enough, and where not much traveling was done between cities that would have a different *local mean time*.

With the advance of the railroads in the 19th century a more common time was needed to avoid confusion in railroad schedules. At that time the railroad's time was often the local mean time of the railroad's headquarters, but when the railroad companies started to connect their networks this was no longer workable. In the mid-19th century the British railways standardized timekeeping by agreeing to use *Greenwich Mean Time* (GMT) that later became an important time reference. The U.S. followed later and in the end of the 19th century a conference established the system of timezones with offsets from Greenwich. Twenty-four time zones were created; each consisting of on average 15° longitudinal degrees wide zone and all one hour apart. However, the timezone boundaries are not straight, to account for local preferences, and in some cases the *GMT offset* is not a whole hour either. The boundaries of the standard time zones continue to change as well.

Figure 1.1 shows the differences between *true solar time*, *mean solar time* and *timezone'd time* for Skien in Norway. It is centered on standardized time (Timezone'd Time in the graph) −− a whole amount of hours' offset from UTC that belongs to the geographical location. In this case that is UTC+1. The "True Solar Time" line shows when the Sun is exactly in the south, where as the "Local Mean Time" line shows the time when the Sun is in the south *on average*.

During the first World War the concept of *Daylight Savings Time* (DST) was introduced, however, the concept was coined much earlier by Benjamin Franklin as early as the late 18th century when he was an American envoy to France. [1] At that time, however, nobody saw any merit in his proposal. William Willet rediscovered DST in the early 20th century. He voraciously tried to convince British parliament to adopt the concept of moving the clocks forwards during summer, until his death in 1915.

Starting with the summer of 1916, a few European countries moved the clock one hour forward to make more efficient use of daylight. The scheme was also briefly in effect in the US of the final years of World War I, while some areas continued using DST until a bit later. During World War II a similar scheme was in effect in the US from 1942 to 1945. After World War II there was no federal law in the US, and every

---

[1] Source: David S. Prerau, *Seize the Daylight*

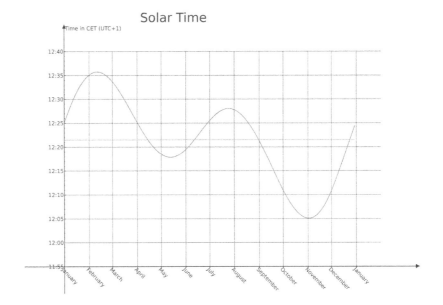

Figure 1.1

state or county was free to choose when to start and end DST, and whether to use it at all. This caused major confusion for transportation schedules and in 1966 congress ended this madness by passing a law that stated that states could chose whether to have DST or not, but that DST had to begin on the last Sunday of April and to end on the last Sunday of October. Updates on this law were made a few times; the most recent in 2007 where DST was set to begin at 2:00 a.m. on the second Sunday of March and end at 2:00 a.m. on the first Sunday of November. Newer amendments to the law also allow for states to exempt certain counties from following DST or not. This mostly shows in Indiana which has an "interesting" history when it comes to DST. Examples in later sections will show the confusing situation for Indiana. The resource previously cited (*Seize the Daylight*) has extensive information on the history of Daylight Savings Time, and also a little bit on the introduction of time zones in general.

Other countries have various different rules regarding whether or not to use DST, and when to begin and end DST. For example, the DST for countries in the European

Union begins at 1:00 a.m. GMT on the last Sunday of March and ends at 1:00 a.m. GMT on the last Sunday of October. Other countries such as Argentina and Brazil determine each year on when, and whether, they want to adopt DST.

With DST added to the mix, there are now three different modifications against local solar time. First, there is *mean solar time* which deviates from *local solar time* by calculating the length of a day over the course of a year and defining "noon" as the average of when the Sun would be in the south. Second, the introduction of *time zones* allows local time to deviate with one hour increments from GMT (or actually UTC, but we'll come back to that later) only. Third, the introduction of *daylight savings time* modifies *standard time* by advancing the clocks during the summer. The first of the two above mentioned differences are shown in Figure 1.1.

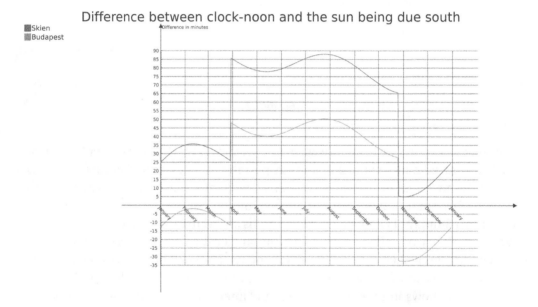

Figure 1.2

The difference between the "True Solar Time" and when the clock strikes twelve is displayed in Figure 1.2. The diagram shows the difference for both Skien, Norway (9.62°E) and Budapest, Hungary (19.04°E).

Calendars

A small note on calendars is required as well. There are many different calendars, some based on the lunar cycle, others on the solar cycle. Currently most people will understand the Gregorian calendar. The Gregorian calendar is a modified version of the Julian calendar. The original Julian calendar has been in effect since around 45 BC. This calendar defines a leap year every four years—February 29th—as an attempt to be as close as possible to the length of the tropical year. A tropical year is defined as the time it takes for the Sun to be in the same position in the cycle of seasons as seen from Earth. The current length of the tropical year is about 365.24219 days (where a day is defined here as 86400 SI seconds). The average length of the Julian year is 365.25 days, which caused notable difference for the start of spring in the 16th century.

The pope commissioned the new Gregorian calendar which defines a leap day every 4 years, except when it is divisible by 100; however, years that are divisible by 400 do have a leap day. The leap day is still on February 29th. The adjustments to when to have a leap year, changes the length of a Gregorian year to 365.2425 days, which is much closer to the length of the tropical year then the Julian year was. Starting in 1582, the different countries started to adopt the Gregorian calendar. For many countries there are 10 days missing. In Italy the calendar jumped from Thursday, 4 October 1582 to Friday, 15 October 1582. Other countries adopted the new calendar later. Sweden however thought up their own scheme of switching to the new calendar, but gave up on their scheme and had to include the unique day February 30th in the year 1712. It is possible to use the Gregorian calendar even for years before people switched from the Julian calendar—this is called the proleptic Gregorian calendar. Concerning PHP, the only calendar that is used is the ISO 8601 calendar. This calendar is the same as the proleptic Gregorian calendar, except for years before the year 1. In the proleptic Gregorian calendar there is no year 0, whereas that year does exist in the ISO 8601 calendar. This makes year -1 in the ISO 8601 calendar the same as 2 BC in the proleptic Gregorian calendar, and year 0 in the ISO 8601 calendar the same as 1 BC in the proleptic Gregorian calendar.

Time Standards

Local time is often shown as "time ± GMT offset", where "time" could be either in 12 or 24-hour representation. Because the 12-hour notation can be confusing regarding midnight and noon, the 24-hour notation is the one used in this book. The 24-hour notation is also called "military time" or "astronomical time". An additional benefit of using the 24-hour notation is that it is understood in every region without having to translate the "a.m." and "p.m." bits. The timezone is often represented by the GMT offset, however this name is not correct. GMT (Greenwich Mean Time) is the **name** of a timezone, as used by the UK during winter times. It would be more correct to use the offset as offset to UTC^2 (*Coordinated Universal Time*). The reason for that is because UTC replaced GMT in 1972 as the basis for the main reference time scale. At this same moment *UT* (*Universal Time*) was created as a continuation of GMT using Earth rotation dynamics as base for a timescale (the mean solar time).

Each UTC day is divided in 24 hours of 60 minutes of 60 seconds (86400 seconds) for each day. The *second* is the SI base unit of time, and defined as a duration of a physical process. Unfortunately a day is not exactly 86400 seconds and in order to keep UTC close to UT a leap second is sometimes added at the end of either June or December.[3] As this is done after actually measuring the difference between UT and UTC, leap seconds can not be predicted.

When a leap second is introduced, the time 23:59:59 is followed by 23:59:60. Theoretically it also possible to skip the last second of a day (23:59:59) but this has not been necessary so far. There is also an additional standard (*TAI*, *International Atomic Time*) which does not include leap seconds like UTC but instead always uses 86400 SI seconds in a day. Over the past decades UTC and TAI slowly drifted apart from the 10 initial seconds in 1972 to the 33 seconds now (and 34 seconds from January 1st,

---

[2]The phrase "Coordinated Universal Time" has the abbreviation "UTC" because when UTC was instituted in 1972 the International Telecommunication Union wanted the same abbreviation for all languages to avoid confusion. As neither the French or English speaking representatives wanted to adopt the abbreviation of the other language (CUT for English, and TUC for French), the compromise UTC was agreed upon.

[3]There are currently some discussions going on regarding the abolishment of leap seconds in UTC, see http://tycho.usno.navy.mil/Discontinuance_of_Leap_Second_Adjustments.pdf for more information.

2009), due to the addition of leap seconds in UTC. This might look like a technicality, but unfortunately it does have an effect of handling time in PHP.

PHP uses the *Unix time stamp* for most of its internal calculations. A Unix time stamp is neither UTC, as it does not support the leap second representation, nor is it similar to TAI, as it uses the concept of UTC days but with a fixed length of 86400 seconds. The epoch of the Unix time stamp is 1970-01-01 00:00:00 UTC[4]. This second is assigned number 0. Each day adds 86400 to this number. For example, "2005-12-31 23:59:00 UTC" would have as Unix time stamp the value 1136073540 (which is 13148 days of 86400 seconds, plus 23 hours of 3600 seconds, plus 59 minutes of 60 seconds). 59 seconds later, the Unix time stamp is 1136073599. At the end of 2005-12-31 a leap second was added to create the UTC time "2005-12-31 23:59:60", which converts to the Unix time stamp 1136073600 just like "2006-01-01 00:00:00" would convert to this number. This means that the time stamp 1136073600 is ambiguous and could mean either second. PHP would have the possibility to account for this fact and make the time stamp it uses count the **number of seconds** as opposed to the **number of days** times 86400 mantra that Unix time stamps use. However, this would cause too many strange issues and therefore PHP ignores leap seconds, just like most operating systems.

Time Stamp Range

Traditionally, the *time_t* data type from the C-language is used to store the Unix time stamp. In many operating systems this data type is defined as "long int" which often means a signed 32-bit integer, although some operating systems (such as Windows) sometimes use an **unsigned** 32-bit integer. The range of a Unix time stamp when stored in a 32-bit signed integer encompasses the seconds between 1901-12-13 20:45:52 UTC and 2038-01-19 03:14:07. On newer (64-bit) processors the "long int" data type contains a 64-bit integer. If the operating system supports this as well, even

---

[4]As date representation this book will use the ISO 8601 date format "YYYY-MM-DD" to prevent confusion about which of the three elements is the month or the day. Because of similar reasons, all times in this book are in 24 hour notation—unless 12 hour notation is required as example. In case both date and time information is present, the full ISO 8601 format is used. An example of date/time information in the full format is "2008-01-13T00:00:00+01:00". There is the date format ("YYYY-MM-DD"), followed by a "T", followed by the time ("HH:ii:ss") and then the UTC offset ("+HH:ii").

PHP's older functions will correctly deal with time stamps in this extended range. In case a 32-bit processor is used, or the operating system still only supports the 32-bit range (or a limitation of it), only PHP's newer APIs overcome this limitation. PHP's newer API functions and methods internally store the Unix time stamp always as a 64-bit signed integer, extending the original 138 year range to encompass time from 290 billion years ago, to 290 billion years in the future—not likely going to be a problem.

Timezones

With the introduction of timezones in the 19th century things got a lot easier compared to the time when *local mean time* was still in use. The new zones in each country/region were assigned names to identify them. In the US the names are for example *Eastern Standard Time, Central Standard Time, Mountain Standard Time* and *Pacific Standard Time*. Because those names are quite long, abbreviations are normally used to designate a time in a specific timezone. Take for example *14:45 CET*, which stands for *14:45 Central European Time*. The aforementioned timezones in the USA and Canada have the following default abbreviations: *EST, CST, MST* and *PST*. When daylight savings time is in effect, the abbreviations often change. *CET* becomes *CEST* (*Central European Summer Time*), *EST* becomes *EDT* (*Eastern Daylight Time*) etc. Unfortunately, just the time and the abbreviation are not unique enough. *17:00 PST* can, for example, mean both *17:00 Pacific Standard Time*, *17:00 Pakistan Standard Time* and even *17:00 Philippine Standard Time*. The abbreviation has a different meaning depending on context. The same timezone can also have different abbreviations, even for the same time. For example in the Netherlands the timezone abbreviation *MEZT* is sometimes used in literature instead of the more common *CEST*—it is merely a localization of the timezone name. Because of those ambiguities, using a timezone abbreviation for identification of a timezone does not work.

An abbreviation does raise some logic issues as well. Over the course of time, there are many places where the timezone rules, and also the timezone abbreviation changed. Knox County in Indiana for example went through many different rule sets:

- from 1953 to 1964 it used Central Time, with daylight savings time (CST and CDT)

- from 1964 to 1969 it used Eastern Time, without using daylight savings time (EST)

- from 1969 to 1970 it used Eastern Time, with daylight savings time (EST and EDT)

- from 1970 to 2006 it used Eastern Time, without using daylight savings time (EST)

- from 2006 to 2007 it used Central Time, with daylight savings time (CST and CDT)

- from 2007 until the next change, it uses Eastern Time, with daylight savings time (EST and EDT)

In this extreme example, there are six different periods with different rules.

To identify this set of rules for this area a unique identifier exists: *America/Indiana/Vincennes* (with Vincennes being the most populous city in the county). These unique identifiers are defined in the *Olson database*, which contains the rules for which UTC offset is used in an area, and with which abbreviation. The Olson database contains information for more than 500 geographical areas. The database also contains most historical information for each different area, sometimes going back as far as the early 20th century. As the database contains rules for when Daylight Savings Time starts, as opposed to the precise moments, it also provides future information about offset changes.

PHP uses this Olson database for all its timezone related date/time operations, just like most Unix based systems (Linux, Mac OS X, FreeBSD etc.). While in older versions PHP simply relied on the operating system to do timezone calculations, in newer versions (since PHP 5.1), PHP does the calculations internally. This allows for much better control of, and thus many more features related to, timezones. The previous situation caused problems on Unix-like systems, where the rule sets could be incomplete, outdated or completely wrong. Windows does not even keep historical data in its timezone and daylight savings time rule database.

Configuring PHP's Timezone

In order to handle the local timezone and daylight savings time rules, PHP needs to know the default timezone of the server. This is specified with the php.ini directive *date.timezone*. This setting **should be** made so that PHP does not have to attempt to guess in which timezone the server is in. The guessing on Unix systems done through a combination of the non-unique timezone abbreviation in combination with the UTC offset and whether daylight savings time (DST) is in effect. This allows for fairly accurate guessing, but it is not 100% accurate. On Windows it is less accurate as only the UTC offset and whether DST is enabled can be obtained reliably from the operating system.

Because the guessing is not 100% accurate and can be slow, it is advised to **always** set the php.ini directive date.timezone. The value for this setting is one of the timezone identifiers as provided by the Olson database. The timezone identifiers are documented in the PHP manual at http://php.net/timezones. There are nine main geographic areas (America, Antarctica, Arctic, Asia, Atlantic, Australia, Europe, Indian and Pacific) and an "Others" group. This last group contains entries that only exist for backward compatibility reasons and should **not** be used, even though the entries might look tempting. All of the available entries in the "Others" group either don't take care of DST change-overs, or contain outdated DST change-over rules. The only safe timezone identifier in this group is "UTC". The other groups contain timezone identifiers for all the major geographic areas. To pick the correct one, you pick the name which matches your area the closest logically - *not geographically*. For example Dutch PHP users should use the identifier "Europe/Amsterdam". In most cases, the name to pick is *Continent / Capital of your country*, but there are a few exceptions in places where either historically or currently the rules are different locally.

Whenever you have error reporting set to E_ALL | E_STRICT PHP will issue a warning when you do not have the date.timezone setting configured properly. The warning looks like: Warning: strtotime(): It is not safe to rely on the system's timezone settings. You are *required* to use the date.timezone setting or the date_default_timezone_set() function. In case you used any of those methods and you are still getting this warning, you most likely misspelled the timezone identifier. We selected Europe/Berlin for CET/1.0/no DST instead in the sample script `strtotime1.php`. Chapter 3 will go deeper into timezones, and how to handle them efficiently in PHP.

Timezone Database

Many times a year the Olson timezone database is updated. PHP allows you to update this database separately from PHP itself with the *timezonedb* PECL extension. This extension provides a drop-in replacement for PHP's built-in timezone database. Please refer to the Appendix A Section on "Upgrading the Timezone Database" for installation instructions. Information on querying the contents of either the built-in database, or a replacement database, can be found in Chapter 3.

Chapter 2

Parsing Date/Time Strings

One of the tasks that developers often have to do with date/times, is parse strings containing date and time information. Computer languages can't really handle things like "January 13th, 2008" directly, and need this information converted into something logical. I explicitly use the word logical here, as strings containing date and time information are everything but logical. Depending on the context, the same string could represent different date/time information[1]

Parsing Strings Containing Time Information

PHP implements the `strtotime()` function, which description reads "Parse about any English textual datetime description into a Unix timestamp"[2]. The return value of this function is an integer containing a Unix time stamp. This function was introduced years ago and has been in PHP at least since PHP 4. For PHP 5.1 and later versions, this function has a new implementation that understands many more formats than before. To use it you can simple provide the function a string containing *time information.* The example in the following code shows the `strtotime()` function applied to the string "January 13th, 2008".

---

[1] From now on I will use "time information" when talking about everything that contains information about dates, times and timezones.

[2] As written in the PHP Manual, by the PHP Documentation Group at `http://php.net`

```
<? php
echo strtotime ("January 13th , 2008"), "\n";
?>
```

The output of this example is 1200178800. In order to see a more meaningful result, we will use the date() function. This function is further described in Chapter 4. For now, we will only be using it in the form of date('c', $value); to show the result of a parsing action. We tie this new date() function call into the previous script in the following code:

```
<? php
$value = strtotime("January 13th , 2008");
echo date ('c', $value), "\n";
?>
```

Running this example with the c modifier, produces the output 2008-01-13T00:00:00+01:00. The output might be different for you, as the last bit (+01:00) depends on which timezone you have configured through the date.timezone php.ini setting. See Chapter 1 for more information on how to configure PHP to use the correct timezone for you. From now on this book expects you to have this configured properly. The author of this book has this date.timezone php.ini setting set to "Europe/Oslo", so in order to get similar results in the examples, you can change your setting to match this value.

The power of the strtotime() function is that it can recognize many different formats automatically. It contains an intelligent parser that manages to figure out many different formats in which time information can be represented. The parser is implemented as an re2c[3] parser, which defines many rules for formats. The main blocks it can recognize are date information, time information and timezone information. A few more complex formats such as the SOAP, XML RPC and Common Log Format are supported as well.

In order to understand what the parser can actually parse, we should examine the parser in slightly more detail. The parser first defines a bunch of simple tokens that can make up a date, time or timezone information string. For example, for times, the parser defines hour24 as token to represent the hours from 0 to 24. While there

---

[3] re2c is a tool to generate parsers.

is another token, hour24lz, which also record the hours from 0 to 24, but requires a leading zero to be present. There are similar tokens for minutes, seconds, meridians, days, years and months (both numeric and textual). From those basic tokens, larger units are composed that usually make up a whole date or time format. For time information there is for example timeshort12 that matches the string "12:00 a.m.". Another example is iso8601normtz that matches the string "20:38:43 +02:00". For date information there is the token datetextual that matches "January 23rd, 2008". The special formats, such as SOAP, also have their own definition-- the token soap matches the format "2008-01-23T20:40:31.1231+04:30". All the compound tokens have parsing rules attached to them that define what to do with the matched data. In this phase the matched tokens are broken apart into the information that describes a day, a month, a minute etc. Appendix C describes all formats that are understood by the parser. The example in the following code shows a few more strings that the parser understands.

```php
<?php
// normal "american" format
echo date( 'c', strtotime( '1/23/08 9:17 pm' ) ), "\n";

// ISO date and 24 hour time
echo date( 'c', strtotime( '2008-12-22 21:29:09' ) ), "\n";

// Common Log Format
echo date( 'c', strtotime( '07/Mar/2008:09:18:31 -0700' ) ), "\n";

// ISO week and week day
echo date( 'c', strtotime( '2008-W04-3' ) ), "\n";
?>
```

When run, this script returns:

```
2008-01-23T21:17:00+01:00
2008-12-22T21:29:09+01:00
2008-03-07T17:18:31+01:00
2008-01-23T00:00:00+01:00
```

As you can see, the output of the third strtotime() call does **not** display the UTC offset that was present in the time information string (-0700), but instead it shows the current UTC offset from the default timezone (+01:00). This is because the return value from strtotime() is always just an integer representing a Unix time stamp, without any other information attached to it. Even if strtotime() would return more than this integer, the date() function would not understand it, as it only accepts an integer as well.

Each of the three information groups (date, time and timezone) can usually only be present once in the string. An error is raised if the same information is present multiple times. strtotime() returns false in those cases.

For timezones, the parser's behavior is less strict. In some cases strings containing time information as encountered "in the wild" contain two timezone specifications. A common format that exhibits this is "Sun, 21 Dec 2003 20:38:33 +0000 GMT". Instead of allowing just one timezone in the string, the parser allows two of them. The second timezone specifier is just ignored, and a warning will be added to the parser output. strtotime() ignores warnings however. The following code shows six different strings with time information.

```php
<?php
// One timezone specifier
echo date( 'c', strtotime( '2008-01-29 20:16:19 +01:00' ) ), "\n";
echo date( 'c', strtotime( '2008-01-29 20:16:19 GMT+01:00' ) ), "\n";

// Two timezone specifiers
echo date( 'c', strtotime( '2008-01-29 20:16:19 GMT +01:00' ) ), "\n";
echo date( 'c', strtotime( '2008-01-29 20:16:19 +0100 GMT' ) ), "\n";
echo date( 'c', strtotime( '2008-01-29 20:16:19 GMT+01:00 Europe/Oslo' ) ), "\n"
    ;

// Three timezone specifiers
echo date( 'c', strtotime( '2008-01-29 20:16:19 GMT +01:00 Europe/Oslo' ) ), "\n
    ";
?>
```

When run, this script returns:

```
2008-01-29T20:16:19+01:00
2008-01-29T20:16:19+01:00
2008-01-29T21:16:19+01:00
2008-01-29T20:16:19+01:00
2008-01-29T20:16:19+01:00
```

```
1970-01-01T01:00:00+01:00
```

In the first two strings, there is only one timezone specifier. GMT+01:00 is a compound one where the GMT bit is simply ignored. In the next three strings, there are two timezone specifiers. In each of the strings, the second timezone is ignored. In the first of the three, the first timezone that is found is GMT. Because the default timezone is set to "Europe/Oslo" (UTC+1) the output is one hour later. The other two are both +01:00 and will therefore show 20:16:19 as time. In the last string there are three timezone specifiers, respectively GMT, +01:00 and Europe/Oslo. Because there are more than two, the parser raises an error condition which results in strtotime() to return false.

There is another exception. The four digit number that the gnunocolon token matches, is interpreted as hours and minutes. If however the same token is found for the second time, it is interpreted as a four digit year. With more than two occurrences an error is thrown and strtotime() returns false. The following code shows this behavior.

```php
<?php
echo date( 'c', strtotime( '1100' ) ), "\n";
echo date( 'c', strtotime( '1100 1984' ) ), "\n";
echo date( 'c', strtotime( '1100 1984 4925' ) ), "\n";
var_dump( strtotime( '1100 1984 4925' ) );
?>
```

When run, this script returns:

```
2008-01-29T11:00:00+01:00
1984-01-29T11:00:00+01:00
1970-01-01T01:00:00+01:00
bool(false)
```

A problem with the strtotime() function is that the range of its return value depends on the Operating System and processor as explained in Chapter 1. To overcome this problem, and the problem that the strtotime() function loses all timezone information as mentioned earlier, the date_create() function was introduced in PHP 5.2. We will get back to the date_create() function later in this chapter.

Other Ways of Creating a Timestamp

strtotime() is not the only way of creating a time stamp out of some form of date/-time information. The mktime() function accepts hour, minute, second, month, day, year and whether DST is/should be used, as arguments. Each of the arguments is an integer. Every argument (besides the DST one) is considered to be the current value if it is omitted. All of the arguments are optional. The following code uses mktime() to modify the current time.

```php
<?php
// current time
echo date( 'c' ), "\n";
// change current hour only
echo date( 'c', mktime( 14 ) ), "\n";
// change hour, minute and seconds
echo date( 'c', mktime( 14, 58, 27 ) ), "\n";
?>
```

When run, this script returns:

```
2008-07-26T12:13:02+02:00
2008-07-26T14:13:02+02:00
2008-07-26T14:58:27+02:00
```

Creating time stamps for just dates with mktime() can be cumbersome too, as is illustrated in the following code. Because the date arguments come after the time arguments, you always have specify the time bits as well. On top of that, the function expects arguments in the "American" order: month, day and year.

```php
<?php
// current time
echo date( 'c' ), "\n";
// change current month and day, reset time
echo date( 'c', mktime( 0, 0, 0, 12, 22 ) ), "\n";
// change only the current day
echo date( 'c', mktime( 0, 0, 0, date( 'm' ), 17 ) ), "\n";
?>
```

When run, this script returns:

```
2008-07-26T12:18:23+02:00
2008-12-22T00:00:00+01:00
2008-07-17T00:00:00+02:00
```

The only parameter that we've not covered yet is the `is_dst` argument to `mktime()`. By default its value is `-1`—meaning that the `mktime()` function sorts out whether the date is in DST or not itself. However, you can change how `mktime()` interprets DST. By specifying a value of `0` you force the function to interpret the passed date/time as being *not* during DST. If you pass a `1` you force it to be interpreted as being *during* DST. The forcing of interpretation can provide somewhat unexpected results as we can see in the following code.

```php
<?php
error_reporting( E_ALL & ~E_DEPRECATED );
// DST is in effect
// default
echo date( 'c', mktime( 15, 8, 58, 7, 26, 2008 ) ), "\n";
echo date( 'c', mktime( 15, 8, 58, 7, 26, 2008, -1 ) ), "\n";

// forced to be interpreted as outside DST
echo date( 'c', mktime( 15, 8, 58, 7, 26, 2008,  0 ) ), "\n";

// forced to be interpreted as inside DST
echo date( 'c', mktime( 15, 8, 58, 7, 26, 2008,  1 ) ), "\n\n";

// DST is not in effect
// default
echo date( 'c', mktime( 9, 15, 0, 12, 22, 2008 ) ), "\n";
echo date( 'c', mktime( 9, 15, 0, 12, 22, 2008, -1 ) ), "\n";

// forced to be interpreted as outside DST
echo date( 'c', mktime( 9, 15, 0, 12, 22, 2008,  0 ) ), "\n";

// forced to be interpreted as inside DST
echo date( 'c', mktime( 9, 15, 0, 12, 22, 2008,  1 ) ), "\n\n";
?>
```

When run, this script returns:

```
2008-07-26T15:08:58+02:00
2008-07-26T15:08:58+02:00
```

```
2008-07-26T16:08:58+02:00
2008-07-26T15:08:58+02:00

2008-12-22T09:15:00+01:00
2008-12-22T09:15:00+01:00
2008-12-22T09:15:00+01:00
2008-12-22T08:15:00+01:00
```

In the second line in the example, we turn off the E_DEPRECATED error level. Since PHP 5.3 using the is_dst parameter to the mktime() function triggers a warning of this type. In PHP 5.1 and 5.2 an E_STRICT message is shown instead, although this is not part of E_ALL and most likely the message doesn't show up.

The third and eighth dates in the output of the script show that if you force the is_dst argument, the time can be an hour off. If you force the argument to be 0 when the accompanying date is observing DST, the time will be an hour late; if you force the argument to be 1 when the accompanying date is *not* observing DST, the time will be an hour early.

Because *all* the arguments to the mktime() function are optional, you could run mktime() without any arguments to obtain the Unix timestamp of the current date and time, however in those cases PHP will suggest you use the time() function instead if you have E_STRICT error reporting turned on. time() will use less resources than mktime() without arguments, and produces the same result.

Another thing to be careful of is that if you want to get a list of all the month names, the following code might not provide the correct results.

```php
<?php
// consider today's date is July 31st, 2008
for ( $i = 1; $i <= 12; $i++ )
{
    echo date( "F ", mktime( 0, 0, 0, $i ) );
}
?>
```

When run, this script returns (when run on the 31st of a random month):

```
January March March May May July July August October October December December
```

This is of course because the mktime()'s fifth parameter is left to its default—which means it uses the current day-of-month. Because there is no February 31st, or April 31st, PHP applies its generic overflow rules which make mktime() return the name of a month that's following the current one. It's obviously very easy to solve, by using both gmmktime() to avoid DST issues, and using 1 as the fifth argument to the function.

Please also be careful with using "nicely" formatted arguments to mktime()—the following code will not output what you would expect.

```php
<?php
echo date( 'c', mktime( 16, 18, 19, 06, 26, 2008 ) ), "\n";
echo date( 'c', mktime( 16, 18, 19, 07, 26, 2008 ) ), "\n";
echo date( 'c', mktime( 16, 18, 19, 08, 26, 2008 ) ), "\n";
echo date( 'c', mktime( 16, 18, 19, 09, 26, 2008 ) ), "\n";
echo date( 'c', mktime( 16, 18, 19, 10, 26, 2008 ) ), "\n";
?>
```

When run, this script returns:

```
2008-06-26T16:18:19+02:00
2008-07-26T16:18:19+02:00
2007-12-26T16:18:19+01:00
2007-12-26T16:18:19+01:00
2008-10-26T16:18:19+01:00
```

The third and fourth dates are "wrong" because number prepended with a 0 are considered octal numbers in PHP. Because octal 08 and octal 09 do not exist, the value is changed with 0. And the 0-th month of a year, is the last month (December) of the previous year.

This example also shows that it's possible to underflow and overflow arguments to mktime(). You can learn more about this later in this chapter.

Using mktime() for UTC Times

There is also a variant of the mktime() function—gmmktime()—that interprets all arguments as if the current timezone was UTC.

The following flaws can be identified with the mktime() function:

- In order to change the date, you also need to set the time elements again.

- The arguments to set the date are in an inconvenient order.

- It is timezone unaware.

PHP's date/time support has solutions for all of these problems in different classes and methods. You will find those later on in this book.

Creating a DateTime Object

The date_create() function accepts the same strings with time information as strtotime(). The major difference is that the date_create() function does not simply return an integer representing a Unix time stamp. The function returns an object that also contains timezone specific information, as well as a broken down version of the time information. Instead of using the date_create() function you can do exactly the same in an OO fashion by using new DateTime().[4] The following code sample shows both methods in action.

```php
<?php
$date = date_create( "2008-01-30 18:42:50 Europe/Oslo" );
$date = new DateTime( "2008-01-30 18:42:50 Europe/Oslo" );
?>
```

Because the function and the object instantiation both return an object, the date() function which we used previously to format a time stamp can no longer be used. Instead, we can obtain the time stamp from the object with the getTimestamp() method. The resulting time stamp can then be fed into the date() function again, like in the following code. Alternatively we could use the date_timestamp_get() function to obtain this time stamp.

---

[4]All of the functions in the date extension have both an OO and a procedural interface. From now on we will use the OO interface in all examples, and mention the equivalent procedural function in the text. The functions that are equivalent to the method on the object, all take the object as first parameter. This makes for example $dateObj->format('c') equivalent to $date_format($dateObj, 'c').

```php
<?php
$date = date_create( "2008-01-30 17:26:18 -05:00" );
echo date( 'c', $date->getTimestamp() ), "\n";
?>
```

The getTimestamp() function was introduced in PHP 5.3. For older PHP versions, you would need to use $dateObj->format('U') to obtain the Unix time stamp from a DateTime object. After examining the output of this script (2008-01-30T23:26:18+01:00), you will see that the timezone information is still lost when formatting the string, just like before. This is because a time stamp cannot represent a timezone. In order to use the timezone information when displaying the string, another method has to be used. The method format() (or the procedural equivalent date_format()) can be called on the DateTime object directly and does not use an integer time stamp like date(). The method accepts a format string as parameter. The format specifiers are the same as for the date() function and are discussed in Chapter 4. In the following code you see the result after we substitute the date()/getTimestamp() method with the format() method.

```php
<?php
$date = new DateTime( "2008-01-30 17:49:20 -05:00" );
echo $date->format( 'c' ), "\n";

$date = new DateTime( "2008-01-30 23:49:20" );
echo $date->format( 'c' ), "\n";
?>
```

When run, this script returns:

```
2008-01-30T17:49:20-05:00
2008-01-30T23:49:20+01:00
```

Handling Errors While Parsing

Another advantage that the new DateTime method has over the strtotime() function is that it is possible to find out why a specific string failed to parse. Where strtotime() only returns false, the object instantiation method stores the warnings and errors that were created while parsing internally. Those warnings and errors can be queried through the DateTime::getLastErrors() method (or date_get_last_errors()). This functionality is new in PHP 5.3. The following code demonstrates the use of DateTime::getLastErrors().

```php
<?php
try
{
  $date = new DateTime( "1923 UTC | Europe/Oslo Ape" );
}
catch ( Exception $e )
{
  echo $e->getMessage(), "\n";
  var_dump( DateTime::getLastErrors() );
}
?>
```

If you take the Object Oriented approach with new DateTime() the constructor will throw an exception when a parser error occurs. The exception message contains the first parse error (see line 8). The other warnings and errors are then displayed through DateTime::getLastErrors() in line 9. The output of this script is:

```
DateTime::__construct(): Failed to parse time string (1923 UTC | Europe/Oslo Ape
    ) at position 9 (|): Unexpected character
array(4) {
  ["warning_count"]=>
  int(1)
  ["warnings"]=>
  array(1) {
    [11]=>
    string(29) "Double timezone specification"
  }
  ["error_count"]=>
  int(2)
  ["errors"]=>
  array(2) {
    [9]=>
    string(20) "Unexpected character"
    [23]=>
    string(29) "Double timezone specification"
  }
}
```

The warning_count and error_count array elements contain the number of warnings, respectively errors. The other two elements (warnings and errors) contain the actual messages. The key of each array elements that contains the warning or error message is the position in the string where the warning or error occurred.

When the date_create() function parses a string with time information and it encounters an error it will not throw an exception, but instead simply return false. You can still use date_get_last_errors() to see the parser warnings and errors as the following code shows.

```php
<?php
$date = date_create( "22:23 * 2008" );
if ( $date === false )
{
  var_dump( date_get_last_errors() );
}
?>
```

If while parsing a string a date is found that invalid, such as 2008-04-31 (April only has 30 days), an additional entry is added to the return value of date_get_last_errors() and DateTime::getLastErrors(). This warning looks like:

```
["warnings"]=>
array(1) {
  [10]=>
  string(27) "The parsed date was invalid"
}
```

Alternatively you can use the checkdate()function to check whether a specific year, month, day combination is valid. Both the checkdate() function and the mechanism in the parser follow the Gregorian calendar. There will be no warning added if the time part of the string is found invalid, because this case can never happen with the textual date/time string parser.

Handling Timezones While Parsing

Both the DateTime constructor and the date_create() function accept a second parameter besides the string to parse. As second parameter, you can pass an object of the DateTimeZone class, as you can see in the following code.

```
<?php
$date = new DateTime( "2008-01-31 22:30:51",
                      new DateTimeZone( "America/Chicago" ) );
echo $date->format( 'c' ), "\n";

$date = new DateTime( "2008-01-31 22:30:51 UTC",
                      new DateTimeZone( "America/Chicago" ) );
echo $date->format( 'c' ), "\n";
?>
```

This timezone will **only** be used in case the string containing time information does not have a timezone specifier itself. During the second DateTime object creation, the passed timezone is therefore ignored. The output is:

```
2008-01-31T22:30:51-06:00
2008-01-31T22:30:51+00:00
```

In case there is no timezone specifier present in the string containing time information and no timezone object is passed as second parameter, the default timezone will be used following the algorithm that is outlined in Chapter 1.

Obtaining a Detailed Parser Result

In some cases you might want to use the result from the time information parser in different ways besides an integer or a date object. The date/time functionality in PHP allows you to utilize the parser to break up a string with time information into all the different parts (such as year, hour, timezone etc.) that the parser can recognize. For this you can use the date_parse() function.

The function accepts the same formats as both strtotime() and new DateTime(). However, the result is neither an integer nor an object. Instead, the function returns an array with the information that the parser could find in the string. The function will also never return `false` but always shows as much of the parsed result as possible, including all warnings and errors that were found while parsing the string. The following code shows a basic example.

```php
<?php
$res = date_parse( 'February 2nd 15:37' );
var_export( $res );
?>
```

When run, this script returns (slightly reformatted):

```
array (
  'year' => false,
  'month' => 2,
  'day' => 2,
  'hour' => 15,
  'minute' => 37,
  'second' => 0,
  'fraction' => 0,
  'warning_count' => 0,
  'warnings' => array (),
  'error_count' => 0,
  'errors' => array (),
  'is_localtime' => false,
)
```

For each of the date and time fields (year, month, day, hour, minute, second, fraction), an entry exists in the returned array. In case some information is not available, and no default is picked the value of the entry will be `false`, like the `year` entry in the example. Depending on the string with time information, more elements could be part of the returned array.

When relative time has been passed to the `date_parse()` function, a new element `relative` is part of the returned array. This element's value is an array itself, and contains information about each relative element (year, month, etc.). The available elements are:

- *year* - The parsed year, or `false` if not available.

- *month* - The parsed month, or `false` if not available.

- *day* - The parsed day, or `false` if not available.

- *hour* - The parsed hour, or `false` if not available.

- *minute* - The parsed minute, or `false` if not available.

- *second* - The parsed second, or `false` if not available.

- *fraction* - The parsed fraction, or `false` if not available.

- *warning_count* - The number of warnings found while parsing the string.

- *warnings* - An array with all warnings. The key is the position in the string, and the value the error message.

- *error_count* - The number of errors found while parsing the string.

- *errors* - An array with all errors. The key is the position in the string, and the value the error message.

- *is_localtime* - Whether timezone information was present in the string. If the value of this array element is `true` a few more elements will be available too.

- *zone_type (optional)* - What type of zone information was found. Three different types exist: UTC offset (`zone` and `is_dst` will be present), abbreviation (UTC, CET, etc.) (`zone`, `is_dst` and `tz_abbr` will be present), and timezone identifier (`tz_id` will be present). Chapter 3 explains the differences between the types, and how to handle timezones in general.

- *zone (optional)* - Minutes west of UTC.

- *is_dst (optional)* - Whether the parsed abbreviation specifies DST time.

- *tz_abbr (optional)* - The abbreviation (`CEST`).

- *tz_id (optional)* - The timezone identifier (`Europe/Amsterdam`).

- *relative* - Relative time elements that will be applied to normally parsed strings while creating a time stamp. This is an array, for its description see below.

If the `relative` element is present, the contents are an array with the following items:

- *year* - The number of years to add.

- *month* - The number of months to add.

- *day* - The number of days to add.

- *hour* - The number of hours to add.

- *minute* - The number of minutes to add.

- *second* - The number of seconds to add.

- *weekday (optional)* - The week day to which to move to first (0 = Sunday, 1 = Monday, etc.).

- *first_day_of_month (optional)* - Whether the special `first` day of month semantics should be used. (See Chapter 6).

- *last_day_of_month (optional)* - Whether the special `last` day of month semantics should be used. (See Chapter 6).

With these results, it is possible to reconstruct back the original string, however, that I leave as an exercise to the reader.

User Specific Formats

Until now we have only used the built-in parser to analyze time information strings. The built-in parser is only adapted for (American) English representations of time information. Many other formats that represent time informations exist as well, and they will not be understood by the default parser. For example the short date format for Japanese (in Japan) is `yy/mm/dd`—such as `08/02/16`. If this string is used with `new DateTime()` it is incorrectly interpreted as `2016-08-02`. In order to cater to those formats as well, since PHP 5.3, PHP's date time support contains the `DateTime::createFromFormat()`, `date_create_from_format()` and `date_parse_from_format()` functions. The first of the three is a factory method to create a new DateTime object, just like new DateTime() would do. Both the createFromFormat() factory method and the date_create_from_format() function create a new DateTime object. The third function, date_parse_from_format() returns the same result as the date_parse() function would do. In addition to the string containing the time information, all three methods require a format string as the first argument. This format string defines the expected format of the string containing the time information.

The format string consists of format specifiers in the form of letters, that describe time information, and other symbols that specify separators. The format specifiers are modeled after the format specifiers for the date() function (see Chapter 4). To parse the "Japanese" format from the previous paragraph, we use the format y/m/d like in the following code.

```php
<?php
$d = DateTime::createFromFormat( 'y/m/d', '08/02/16' );
echo $d->format( 'c' ), "\n";
?>
```

When run, this script returns:

```
2008-02-16T00:00:00+01:00
```

During parsing with new DateTime() and date_create() all unknown, or unavailable elements are set to the current date/time. This does also happen while parsing from a format. In case you want to reset all the elements to the default (which represents 1970-01-01 00:00:00 in the current default timezone) you can use the ! (exclamation mark) format specifier. Another modifier, the | (pipe character) also allows you to reset certain values in the result. Instead of resetting all values, it will only set the values that have not been parsed yet to the default values. All parsing is done in order, which means that the position of the ! modifier is important. The following script demonstrates this.

```php
<?php
$date = 'America/New_York 2008 02-24';

// all unparsed values are set to the current time
```

```
$d = DateTime::createFromFormat( 'e Y m-d', $date );
echo $d->format( 'c' ), "\n";

// the 'e' (timezone) is ignored as the ! preceding it resets the value
// back to the default timezone.
$d = DateTime::createFromFormat( 'e! Y m-d', $date );
echo $d->format( 'c' ), "\n";

// the 'e' (timezone) and 'Y' are ignored.
$d = DateTime::createFromFormat( 'e Y! m-d', $date );
echo $d->format( 'c' ), "\n";

// nothing is ignored, and all the values that were not set after
// parsing 'e Y' are set to 1970-01-01 00:00:00 in the default timezone.
$d = DateTime::createFromFormat( 'e Y| m-d', $date );
echo $d->format( 'c' ), "\n";
?>
```

When run, this script returns:

```
2008-02-24T08:55:27-05:00
2008-02-24T00:00:00+01:00
1970-02-24T00:00:00+01:00
2008-02-24T00:00:00-05:00
```

There are other modifiers that do not map to a specific value that can be parsed. Those modifiers allow you to define separators and (sets) of random characters. For example, to parse a date in Japanese such as in Figure 2.1, you could use the following format: Y*m*d*.

2008年03月21日
Figure 2.1

The * modifier envelopes a sequence of characters up to the next whitespace, separator or number.

Please be aware that PHP 5 does not deal with multi byte characters, but just with bytes. This means that the Japanese characters (encoding in UTF-8) do not match the ? modifier, which stands for a single "byte". Appendix B lists all possible modifier letters.

The formats do not restrict which values you can pass in—and do not reject the date if one of the values is out of bounds, such as using day number 34. In case numbers are out of bounds, it will be correctly adjusted by modifying the more significant unit. In the example with day number 34 the month will be increased by 1, and the day decreased by 3-6 depending on which month is current. The same happens also for all the other units.

Obtaining a Detailed Parser Result from a User Specified Format

Just as it is possible to only parse a date with the date_parse() function for the normal parser, there is also an equivalent function for the by-format parser: date_parse_from_format(). It will return the same type of array as output, and accepts the same parameters as date_create_from_format(). While parsing the date string, there is no need to fill-in unparsed elements. Therefore the date_parse_from_format() function will use false as value for any element that has not been parsed by the function. The only exception here is that if any of the time elements (hour, minute, seconds) are parsed, the other time elements are reset to 0 if they were not present. The following code demonstrates this.

```php
<?php
$date = 'America/New_York 2008 02 24';

$d = date_parse_from_format( 'e Y m i', $date );
var_dump( $d );
?>
```

The output of this script shows that the day element is still false, but the others (year, month, hour, minute and second) either have the parsed value, or are reset to 0. The reset modifiers (! and |) have the same effect as when they're used when creating a DateTime object from a string by format.

The parse-by-format parser will add elements to the warnings array when it encounters an invalid date, just like the normal textual date/time string parser does. Unlike the textual parser, it will also do this for invalid time strings—something that can not happen with the textual parser.

Parser Quirks

The parser has a couple of quirks that can be confusing if you're not aware of them. This section tries to address those quirks.

Parsing Order

While scanning the string with time information, the parser goes from left to right through the string. This is important when keywords such as "today" and "tomorrow" are used. Along with "yesterday", "now", "noon" and "midnight" those keywords will reset the already parsed time.

The following code shows the differences that occur when the order of items in the string is reversed.

```php
<?php
echo date( 'c', strtotime( 'tomorrow 11:00' ) ), "\n";
echo date( 'c', strtotime( '11:00 tomorrow' ) ), "\n";
?>
```

When run, this script returns:

```
2008-01-22T11:00:00+01:00
2008-01-22T00:00:00+01:00
```

The first line shows 11:00 of the next day like expected, but the second line shows midnight of tomorrow (the next day).

Time Stamps Have Implicit Timezone

When you parse a time stamp with the @ marker with either date_create() or new DateTime() you will notice that the timezone UTC is automatically attached to the returned DateTime object.

The following code demonstrates this.

```php
<?php
// parse the timestamp
$d = date_create( '@1201124017' );
```

```
echo $d->format( 'c' ), "\n";

// parse the timestamp with UTC offset in string
$d = date_create( '@1201124017 +04:00' );
echo $d->format( 'c' ), "\n";

// parse the timestamp with timezone atttached
$d = date_create( '@1201124017', timezone_open( 'Europe/Helsinki' ) );
echo $d->format( 'c' ), "\n";
?>
```

In all three cases, the output will be 2008-01-23T21:33:37+00:00.

Parsing Times That Do Not Exist

When time jumps from "normal" time to "Daylight Savings Time" there will be an hour "missing". The hour goes missing because time jumps an hour forwards. For example in Oslo, DST starts at March 30, 2008, at 02:00. After 01:59:59 CET will then follow 03:00:00 CEST. The time "02:20" does not exist in this time zone. PHP however, will allow this to be parsed, and will automatically advance the clock with the amount that the DST change adds to normal time (this is not always an hour). This is demonstrated in the following code.

```
<?php
echo date( 'c', strtotime( '2008-03-30 01:59:59 Europe/Oslo' ) ), "\n";
echo date( 'c', strtotime( '2008-03-30 02:00:00 Europe/Oslo' ) ), "\n";
echo date( 'c', strtotime( '2008-03-30 02:59:59 Europe/Oslo' ) ), "\n";
echo date( 'c', strtotime( '2008-03-30 03:00:00 Europe/Oslo' ) ), "\n";
?>
```

When run, this script returns:

```
2008-03-30T01:59:59+01:00
2008-03-30T03:00:00+02:00
2008-03-30T03:59:59+02:00
2008-03-30T03:00:00+02:00
```

Chapter 3

Dealing with Timezones

As explained in Chapter 1, timezones make handling dates and times really tricky. All the strange rules and exceptions, as well as changes in those rules and exceptions can not be easily expressed as a simple UTC offset, or a timezone abbreviation such as CEST or PDT. Instead the preferred way of describing those rules is with a timezone identifier, such as "America/Los_Angeles," "Europe/Paris" or "Asia/Tokyo". As mentioned in the introduction those identifiers are defined in the "Olson database"—named after the current maintainer Arthur David Olson. PHP utilizes this database internally. It can be upgraded manually as well; see Appendix A.

Different Types of Timezones

Date/time strings might come with one of three different timezone types (or none at all). The simplest one is the UTC offset variant, where the only information stored is the UTC offset in seconds. This type of timezone is found in a string such as 2008-05-12T13:26:11+02:00—the ISO 8601 format. In this example the timezone is 2 hours east of UTC. The range is not from -12 hours to +12 hours difference from UTC, because there are some locations on Earth where the difference is larger than this. At the moment, the range is from -43200 (-12 hours) to 50400 (+14 hours).

The second type is used when an abbreviation is found while parsing a string. An example of this would be Mon May 12 15:02:12 CEST 2008. For this type of timezone, PHP stores the base UTC offset, and whether there is Daylight Savings Time in effect or not. PHP has to make an educated guess however on which offset to attach to such a timezone. An example here is that CEST could mean both a +2 or a +3 hour offset from UTC. The +2 hour offset is the most common one, while the +3 hour offset is only a historical possibility.[1] PHP's date/time library contains a list with priority mappings from abbreviation to UTC offset, and whether DST is enabled or not. It is possible to retrieve this list, by utilizing the DateTimeZone::listAbbreviations() function as you can see in the following code.

```php
<?php
$abbrs = DateTimeZone::listAbbreviations();
foreach ( $abbrs as $abbr => $data )
{
    printf( "%-6s: %6.2f %s\n",
            strtoupper( $abbr ),
            $data[0]['offset'] / 3600,
            $data[0]['dst'] ? ' DST' : '' );
}
?>
```

This script loops over all the timezone abbreviations that PHP knows about and for each one lists the first entry in the array. This is the element that PHP will choose when parsing from a string. You can see from it's output that not all timezones have whole, half or quarter hour offsets from UTC. Take for example PMT—used in Suriname (Paramaribo) in 1934/1935—which has a -3h40m52s offset from UTC. One should be aware however that in some cases you might get an unexpected output. The abbreviation EST is officially used in both the US and in Australia, which obviously have a totally different UTC offset. In the few cases where there are conflicts, PHP makes a choice. For conflicts between US abbreviations and Australian ones, the US ones are used because this is what PHP has done historically.

The third and last type of timezones is the "Timezone Identifier". This identifier is a name like Europe/Amsterdam that contains all the different UTC offsets tied to transition dates. This type is used whenever it's encountered during parsing, or when no explicit timezone was attached to a date/time being parsed. In the latter case the default configured timezone identifier is used.

---

[1]It was in use in 1945 in Kaliningrad only.

Default Timezone

The default timezone depends on a number of factors. If you've followed the advice in the introduction of always setting the php.ini setting date.timezone, then if nothing else is done, this is the current default timezone. There are a few things that can change this.

First of all, you can set the TZ environment variable with something like:

```php
<?php
putenv( "TZ=Europe/Oslo" );
?>
```

Allowing the php.ini setting to be overridden with this TZ environment variable is only supported for backwards compatibility reasons and will not work in PHP 6 anymore. There are multiple issues with using environment variables. One of them is that it affects all threads in a process. Another is that it would also affect the web server that PHP would be running it, and it could thus influence the timezones that Apache uses in its logs.

The second way you can influence the default current timezone is with the date_default_timezone_set() function. This function accepts as its sole parameter a timezone identifier in the same way as the date.timezone php.ini setting. The function allows you to override your default timezone for the duration of your script in case the global setting one is not correct for you, and you cannot (or don't want to) set it with .htaccess.

The current default timezone is used on many occasions. First of all, it will be associated with any DateTime object which was not initialized with a timezone identifier, timezone abbreviation or UTC offset. To see which timezone is associated with a DateTime object you can use the getTimeZone() method. This method extracts the timezone from the DateTime object, and returns it encapsulated in a DateTimeZone object. Only since PHP 5.3 are UTC offset and timezone abbreviation based timezone objects supported with getTimeZone().

One of the methods of the DateTimeZone class is getName(). This function will, depending on the type of timezone, return either the identifier, abbreviation or UTC offset. Abbreviation and UTC offset based timezones are only supported with getName() since PHP 5.3. The example in the following code demonstrates the different possibilities.

```php
<?php
date_default_timezone_set( 'Europe/Oslo' );

// no explicit timezone during initialization, use default
$d = new DateTime( "2008-05-14 20:25" );
$tz = $d->getTimezone();
echo $tz->getName(), "\n";

// explicit timezone identifier during initialization
$d = new DateTime( "2008-05-14 20:25 America/Chicago" );
$tz = $d->getTimezone();
echo $tz->getName(), "\n";

// explicit UTC offset during initialization
$d = new DateTime( "2008-05-14 20:25 +0345" );
$tz = $d->getTimezone();
echo $tz->getName(), "\n";

// explicit timezone abbreviation
$d = new DateTime( "2008-05-14 20:25 PDT" );
$tz = $d->getTimezone();
echo $tz->getName(), "\n";
?>
```

The output of this script is:

```
Europe/Oslo
America/Chicago
+03:45
PDT
```

As you can see from this output, the getName() function's return depends on the type of timezone that is associated. The latter two will always have a fixed UTC offset, while the offset of the first two varies depending on the date/time.

There are a few functions that are influenced by the current default timezone. These functions are the ones that do not deal with DateTime objects directly, but instead interact with Unix timestamps. The formatting functions that are affected are date(), gmdate(), idate(), strftime() and gmstrftime(). new DateTime() and `date_create()` also make use of the default timezone in case no timezone is present in the date/time string.

DateTimeZone

Chapter 2 already showed the `DateTimeZone` object. It was used in the constructor of the `DateTime` class to override the current default timezone with a user defined one. We repeat the example here for clarity:

```
<?php
$date = new DateTime( "2008-01-31 22:30:51",
                      new DateTimeZone( "America/Chicago" ) );
echo $date->format( 'c' ), "\n";

$date = new DateTime( "2008-01-31 22:30:51 UTC",
                      new DateTimeZone( "America/Chicago" ) );
echo $date->format( 'c' ), "\n";
?>
```

The output is again:

```
2008-01-31T22:30:51-06:00
2008-01-31T22:30:51+00:00
```

There is another way that gives you a `DateTimeZone` object. By using the `getTimeZone()` method on a `DateTime` object you will get a `DateTimeZone` object the describes the timezone that belongs to the `DateTime` object. Building on the previous example, we use the `getTimeZone()` method on the just created `DateTime` object in the following code.

```
<?php
$date = new DateTime( "2008-01-31 22:30:51",
                      new DateTimeZone( "America/Chicago" ) );

$timezone = $date->getTimeZone();
var_dump( $timezone );
?>
```

You can reference the code in the previous section for the cases where the DateTimeZone object is obtained from a parsed string.

The DateTimeZone class has a few methods. We've already seen the getName() method earlier in this chapter, as well as the static method DateTimeZone::listAbbreviations(). For those OO methods, there are also procedural versions in the name of timezone_name_get() and timezone_abbreviations_list(). The timezone_name_get() function accepts as the only parameter a DateTimeZone object, while the timezone_abbreviations_list() function does not require any arguments.

The following sections will introduce the other methods that the DateTimeZone class contains.

Getting The Offset Belonging to a Timezone

The DateTimeZone->getOffset() method, or its procedural variant timezone_offset_get(), returns the UTC offset that is valid for this specific timezone at the time that the passed DateTime object specifies. In the following code, we demonstrate that the UTC offset in case of a DateTimeZone from a timezone "identifier" could be different, while the two other types do not depend on which time in the year it is.

```php
<?php
date_default_timezone_set( 'Europe/Oslo' );
$d1 = new DateTime( '2008-01-14 21:43' );
$d2 = new DateTime( '2008-05-14 21:43' );

// UTC offset only
$d = new DateTime( "2008-05-14 20:25 +0345" );
echo $d->getTimezone()->getOffset( $d1 ) / 3600, "\n";
echo $d->getTimezone()->getOffset( $d2 ) / 3600, "\n\n";

// Timezone Abbreviation
$d = new DateTime( "2008-05-14 20:25 PDT" );
echo $d->getTimezone()->getOffset( $d1 ) / 3600, "\n";
echo $d->getTimezone()->getOffset( $d2 ) / 3600, "\n\n";

// Timezone Identifier
$d = new DateTime( "2008-05-14 20:25" );
echo $d->getTimezone()->getOffset( $d1 ) / 3600, "\n";
```

```
echo $d->getTimezone()->getOffset( $d2 ) / 3600, "\n\n";
?>
```

This script outputs:

```
3.75
3.75

-7
-7

1
2
```

This demonstrates that although the abbreviation and UTC offset variants are useful for display, they are not sufficient if you want to deal with the date later on again. The reason for this is that the timezone information that is contained in the first and second examples does not know anything about transition rules for timezones.

Transition Rules in Timezones

A transition rule describes at which point in time a specific UTC-offset is valid for a specific timezone.

Transition rules are only part of DateTimeZone objects that are build from a timezone identifier. This includes DateTimeZone objects created through the constructor with a timezone identifier, and DateTimeZone objects obtained by calling the getTimeZone() method on a DateTime object that was created from a string without any timezone specification or a timezone identifier, like Europe/Amsterdam.

The DateTimeZone->getTransitions() method (or the procedural equivalent timezone_transitions_get() function) allows you to fetch transition times from a DateTimeZone object. The example in the following code first shows that a DateTimeZone object created from a DateTime object without transitions returns no transitions. Secondly it shows an example of the returned array with transitions. We're using the timezone America/Caracas here because it has so few transitions.

```
<?php
date_default_timezone_set( 'America/Caracas' );
```

```
$d = new DateTime( "2008-07-09 21:14:33 CEST" );
$tz = $d->getTimezone();
var_dump( $tz->getTransitions() );

$d = new DateTime( "2008-07-09 21:14:33" );
$tz = $d->getTimezone();
foreach( $tz->getTransitions() as $t )
{
  printf("%30s %6d %s %s (%d)\n", $t['time'], $t['offset'],
      $t['isdst'] ? 'yes' : 'no ', $t['abbr'], $t['ts'] );
}
?>
```

This script outputs:

```
bool(false)
-219246529-01-27T08:29:52+0000 -16060 no  CMT (-9223372036854775808)
        1912-02-12T04:27:40+0000 -16200 no  VET (-1826739140)
        1965-01-01T04:30:00+0000 -14400 no  VET (-157750200)
        2007-12-09T07:00:00+0000 -16200 no  VET (1197183600)
```

This script shows the few different array elements for each transition. There is the
Unix time stamp in the ts element, the ISO 8601 representation in the time element,
the UTC offset in the offset element, the timezone abbreviation used for the period
in which this specific UTC offset is valid in the abbr element and whether this timezone variant is considered as DST in the isdst element.

The earliest transition element that is shown, is for the smallest possible Unix time
stamp that the system supports. For a 64-bit machine like mine, this is very very far
in the past. For a 32-bit machine it is around 1901. The current timezone database
in PHP only stores transition times in 32-bit integers, so there is little use in showing
the transition from 219 million years in the past.[2]

The DateTimeZone::getTransitions() method supports returning transitions for
only a specific time range since PHP 5.3. The example in the following code demonstrates on how to show all transitions between 1980 and 2010.

---

[2]It is likely that the supported range for timezone transition dates will be expanded to the 64-bit
range for all platforms in the future.

```php
<?php
$tz = new DateTimeZone( 'America/Indiana/Vincennes' );

$start = strtotime( '1980-01-01 UTC' );
$end   = strtotime( '2010-01-01 UTC' );

foreach( $tz->getTransitions( $start, $end ) as $t )
{
  printf("%20s %6.1f %s %4s (%d)\n", $t['time'], $t['offset'] / 3600,
      $t['isdst'] ? 'DST' : '   ', $t['abbr'], $t['ts'] );
}
?>
```

When run, this script returns:

```
1980-01-01T00:00:00+0000     -5.0       EST (315532800)
2006-04-02T07:00:00+0000     -5.0 DST   CDT (1143961200)
2006-10-29T07:00:00+0000     -6.0       CST (1162105200)
2007-03-11T08:00:00+0000     -5.0 DST   CDT (1173600000)
2007-11-04T07:00:00+0000     -5.0       EST (1194159600)
2008-03-09T07:00:00+0000     -4.0 DST   EDT (1205046000)
2008-11-02T06:00:00+0000     -5.0       EST (1225605600)
2009-03-08T07:00:00+0000     -4.0 DST   EDT (1236495600)
2009-11-01T06:00:00+0000     -5.0       EST (1257055200)
```

The range can currently only be given in the form of Unix timestamps. It is also possible to only provide the start time stamp argument to the DateTimeZone::getTransitions() method.

Location Information in Timezones

Since PHP 5.3 the timezone database also contains basic location information for each timezone. This information includes the country code, geographical location and additional comments for where this timezone is in use. Obtaining this information is done through the DateTimeZone->getLocation() method. In the following code, the getLocation() method is used to show the location information for the "Europe/Paris" and "America/Indiana/Knox" timezones.

```php
<?php
$paris = new DateTimeZone( "Europe/Paris" );
```

```php
var_dump( $paris->getLocation() );

$indiana = new DateTimeZone( "America/Indiana/Knox" );
echo join( ' - ', array_values( $indiana->getLocation() ) );
?>
```

When run, this script returns:

```
array(4) {
  ["country_code"]=>
  string(2) "FR"
  ["latitude"]=>
  float(48.86666)
  ["longitude"]=>
  float(2.33333)
  ["comments"]=>
  string(0) ""
}
US - 41.29583 - -85.375 - Eastern Time - Indiana - Starke County
```

Positive latitudes are north of the equator, while negative latitudes are south of the equator. Negative longitudes are west of Greenwich and positive longitudes are east of Greenwich. As you can see in the output of the previous listing, there is no comment for "Europe/Paris" but for "America/Indiana/Knox" the comment says "Eastern Time - Indiana - Starke County". Only for more specific timezones will you find a comment.

Associating with DateTime objects

We've already seen the DateTime::getTimeZone() method to create a DateTimeZone object from an existing DateTime object. Of course it is also possible to associate a timezone in the form of a DateTimeZone object with a DateTime object. This is possible with the DateTime::setTimeZone() method (or the procedural equivalent date_timezone_set(). This method takes as its only argument a DateTimeZone object as is illustrated in the following code.

```php
<?php
$tz1 = new DateTimeZone( 'Pacific/Honolulu' );
```

```
$tz2 = new DateTimeZone( 'Asia/Singapore' );

$d = new DateTime( '2008-07-12 08:26 UTC' );
echo $d->format( "Y-m-d H:i:s T (P)" ), "\n";

$d->setTimeZone( $tz1 );
echo $d->format( "Y-m-d H:i:s T (P)" ), "\n";

$d->setTimeZone( $tz2 );
echo $d->format( "Y-m-d H:i:s T (P)" ), "\n";
?>
```

When run, this script returns:

```
2008-07-12 08:26:00 UTC (+00:00)
2008-07-11 22:26:00 HST (-10:00)
2008-07-12 16:26:00 SGT (+08:00)
```

With the setTimeZone() method you can easily change the associated timezone of a DateTime object. However, this means that for further operations on the object this new timezone is used. If you want to avoid that, you need to clone the DateTime object before associating the new timezone. The next example demonstrates that.

```
<?php
$tz1 = new DateTimeZone( 'Africa/Johannesburg' );

// without cloning
$d = new DateTime( '2008-07-12 08:26 UTC' );
echo $d->format( "Y-m-d H:i:s T (P)" ), "\n";
$e = $d;
$e->setTimeZone( $tz1 );
echo $e->format( "Y-m-d H:i:s T (P)" ), "\n";
echo $d->format( "Y-m-d H:i:s T (P)" ), "\n";
echo "\n";

// with cloning
$d = new DateTime( '2008-07-12 08:26 UTC' );
echo $d->format( "Y-m-d H:i:s T (P)" ), "\n";
$e = clone $d;
$e->setTimeZone( $tz1 );
echo $e->format( "Y-m-d H:i:s T (P)" ), "\n";
echo $d->format( "Y-m-d H:i:s T (P)" ), "\n";
```

```
?>
```

When run, this script returns:

```
2008-07-12 08:26:00 UTC (+00:00)
2008-07-12 10:26:00 SAST (+02:00)
2008-07-12 10:26:00 SAST (+02:00)

2008-07-12 08:26:00 UTC (+00:00)
2008-07-12 10:26:00 SAST (+02:00)
2008-07-12 08:26:00 UTC (+00:00)
```

Querying the Timezone Database

All the timezone identifiers such as "Europe/Oslo" and "America/New_York" are defined in the Olson database. This database is used by PHP to provide timezone support. PHP allows you to query the database to find out which timezones are supported with the DateTimeZone::listIdentifiers() static method (or its procedural equivalent timezone_identifiers_list()). Without any arguments this method returns all timezone identifiers, except for the ones that are only available for backwards compatibility reasons. At the moment this list contains about 450 timezones. The following code shows the number of timezones and the first five identifiers.

```php
<?php
$identifiers = DateTimeZone::listIdentifiers();
echo count( $identifiers ), "\n";

foreach( array_slice( $identifiers, 0, 5 ) as $tz )
{
  echo $tz, "\n";
}
?>
```

When run, this script returns something similar to:

```
447
Africa/Abidjan
```

```
Africa/Accra
Africa/Addis_Ababa
Africa/Algiers
Africa/Asmara
```

Letting the users select one timezone out of more than 400 timezones is impractical—both because of user friendliness and technical considerations. It's hard for a user to make a proper choice out of 400+ possible timezones, and it's also a strain on resources to display a select box with 400 items. This is why since PHP 5.3 the `DateTimeZone::listIdentifiers()` method allows an optional argument to restrict the number of returned timezones.

Restricting Timezone Listings by Continent

Each timezone is part of a timezone group, which roughly matches to continents. This is the first part of a timezone identifier—for example the "Europe" in "Europe/Oslo" or the "Asia" in "Asia/Tokyo".

The optional argument that you can pass to the `listIdentifiers()` method is a bit-field that allows you to combine the listing of timezones from the different groups. The date extension defines the constants in the following table for this purpose.

Constant	Description
DateTimeZone::AFRICA	Africa
DateTimeZone::AMERICA	North and South America
DateTimeZone::ANTARCTICA	Antarctic Bases
DateTimeZone::ARCTIC	Only `Arctic/Longyearbyen`
DateTimeZone::ASIA	Asia
DateTimeZone::ATLANTIC	Islands in the Atlantic Ocean
DateTimeZone::AUSTRALIA	Australia
DateTimeZone::EUROPE	Europe
DateTimeZone::INDIAN	Islands in the Indian Ocean
DateTimeZone::PACIFIC	Islands in the Pacific Ocean
DateTimeZone::UTC	The `UTC` timezone

DateTimeZone::ALL	All of the above, without backwards compatibility timezones
DateTimeZone::ALL_WITH_BC	All of the above, including backwards compatibility timezones

The following code shows how to return only the timezones from the `Europe` and `Arctic` regions.

```php
<?php
$identifiers = DateTimeZone::listIdentifiers( DateTimeZone::EUROPE |
    DateTimeZone::ARCTIC );
echo count( $identifiers ), "\n";

foreach( array_slice( $identifiers, 0, 5 ) as $tz )
{
  echo $tz, "\n";
}
?>
```

When run, this script returns something similar to:

```
59
Arctic/Longyearbyen
Europe/Amsterdam
Europe/Andorra
Europe/Athens
Europe/Belfast
```

Aggregating Timezone Listings

The above method already reduces the amount of timezones a user has to pick from in one go. But still, now the user needs to select the continent first. Most of the timezones in Europe are actually not different anymore—there are just different timezone entries because of historical data. Because of this, it might be possible to reduce the list of timezones even further. The following script demonstrates a way to do this. The script has embedded comments to explain what the script does. A few remarks regarding some implementation choices follows.

```php
<?php
// Obtain the current time, we'll use this later to format
// the current time for each of the different timezone
// rules.
$date = new DateTime();

// Get all the timezones, but not the ones from Antarctica.
$zones = timezone_identifiers_list(
  DateTimeZone::ALL & ~DateTimeZone::ANTARCTICA );

// Loop over all the returned zones.
foreach ( $zones as $zone )
{
  // We instantiate the timezone object so we can fetch
  // the definitions from it.
  $tz = new DateTimeZone( $zone );
  // Fetch only the transitions from this point on as
  // we're not intersted in the past.
  $d = timezone_transitions_get( $tz, time() );

  // Find current transition (by finding the next
  // transition).
  foreach ( $d as $idx => $tr ) {
    if ($tr['ts'] > time()) {
      break;
    }
  }

  // From the next transition, deduct the current one if it
  // is different.
  $dnext = $d[$idx];
  $dnow = isset( $d[$idx-1] ) ? $d[$idx-1] : $dnext;

  // Use the timezone object to format the current time
  // for the current zone.
  $date->setTimeZone( $tz );
  $currentTime = $date->format( 'H:i' );

  // Create a key that allows us to aggregate multiple
  // zones into one zone rule.
  $key = sprintf( "%d|%d|%d|%d|%d|%d|%s",
    $dnow['offset'], $dnext['offset'],
    $dnow['ts'], $dnext['ts'],
    $dnow['isdst'], $dnext['isdst'],
    $currentTime
  );
```

```php
  // Add the current zone to the zones array with the key
  // that we've just created.
  $ar[$key][] = $zone;
}

// Sort the array according to the current time.
function sortOffset( $a, $b )
{
  $ap = explode( '|', $a );
  $bp = explode( '|', $b );

  return $ap[6] > $bp[6] ? 1 : -1;
}
uksort( $ar, 'sortOffset' );

// Loop over the sorted array and create a displayable rule
// description containing the locations it consists of.
foreach ( $ar as $key => $value )
{
  // Initialization
  $continent = $descriptions = array();
  $tzId = null;

  // Grab the first two parts of the key, and convert them
  // to hours offset from UTC.
  $parts = explode( '|', $key );
  $offset1 = $parts[0] / 3600;
  $offset2 = $parts[1] / 3600;

  // Select the normal and DST variants of the timezone
  // rule.
  $offsetBase = $parts[4] == 1 ? $offset2 : $offset1;
  $offsetDst = $parts[4] == 0 ? $offset2 : $offset1;

  // Create formatted versions of both the base and DST
  // variants - but the latter only when it differs from
  // the base variant.
  $formattedBaseOffset = sprintf( "%+03d:%02d", $offsetBase,
    abs( $offsetBase - intval( $offsetBase ) ) * 60 );
  $formattedDstOffset = $parts[0] == $parts[1] ? '' :
    sprintf( "/%+03d:%02d", $offsetDst,
      abs( $offsetDst - intval( $offsetDst ) ) * 60 );

  // Create the first part of the description - the
  // current time and the UTC offsets.
```

```
$description = "{$parts[6]} - ";
$description .= "UTC$formattedBaseOffset$formattedDstOffset (";

// Format the locations nicely by grouping them by
// continent, and a special case for UTC that doesn't
// have a / in its timezone identifier.
foreach( $value as $location )
{
  $parts = explode( '/', $location, 2 );
  if ( count( $parts ) == 1 )
  {
    $descriptions[] = 'UTC';
  }
  else
  {
    $continent[$parts[0]][] =
      ucwords( str_replace( '_', ' ', $parts[1] ) );
  }
  // Update the timezone identifier with the last seen
  // location.
  $tzId = $location;
}
foreach( $continent as $contName => $locations )
{
  $descriptions[] = "$contName: ". implode( ', ', $locations );
}
// Add the locations to the description.
$description .= implode( '; ', $descriptions ) . ')';

// Show the description - the accompanying timezone
// identifier is now stored in $tzId.
echo $description, "\n";
echo "\t", $tzId, "\n";
}
?>
```

In lines 8 and 9, we use the argument to `timezone_identifiers_list()` method, which is new in PHP 5.3. To make this script work with PHP 5.2, simply remove the arguments to the function.

In line 19, we also use a feature that is new in PHP 5.3. For PHP 5.2, simply leave away the second argument to `timezone_transitions_get()`.

Lines 41 to 46 generate a key. This key will be the same for every timezone identifier that has the same base and DST UTC-offsets, and the same transition times from/to DST. The other three parts of the key are not really adding anything to the uniqueness, but merely provide additional data which is used later in the script.

The function in lines 54-60, and the uksort() call in line 61 sort the array according to the current time. Alternatively you could sort on the base UTC-offset. For this you need to use the fifth and sixth part of the key to find out which of the first two parts is the base UTC-offset, and which is the DST UTC-offset. However, it is most likely easier for users to find the correct entry in the list by looking for their current time. And this is what the sorting function in the script above does.

In lines 108-109, we convert the timezone identifier to a presentable name. Please be aware that there could be duplicates, because the spelling of names in the database changed, or because there are some backwards compatible names in the database. Please also note that the timezone identifiers are generally not meant to be shown to the user—however, it functions fine in the constrains of this script.

In the last two lines, 124-125, we display the generated description, as well as the timezone identifier that can be used to specify the rules belonging to the description. This identifier is the name of the last location that was found under a specific key—by no means the most logical one. Instead of displaying the description and the timezone identifier, it is probably best to return an array where the key is the timezone identifier and the value the description. This array can then be rendered as a select box for example. It is probably also wise to cache this array as running the algorithm in this script could be very intensive if it was run for every request.

Listing Timezone Identifiers By Country

Most countries have just one timezone, and thus one timezone identifier would be adequate in those cases. Since PHP 5.3 it is possible to list all the timezone identifiers that are active in one country. For this we use the DateTimeZone::listIdentifiers() method again. Instead of specifying the continent with a constant, we use DateTimeZone::PER_COUNTRY as first argument to the method. The second argument now specifies the ISO 3166-1 two-character country code to list identifiers. The example in the following code shows how to use this feature.

```php
<?php
echo "USA:\n";
$us = DateTimeZone::listIdentifiers( DateTimeZone::PER_COUNTRY, "US" );
```

```
echo wordwrap( join( " ", $us ), 66 );

echo "\n\nChina:\n";
$cn = DateTimeZone::listIdentifiers( DateTimeZone::PER_COUNTRY, "CN" );
echo wordwrap( join( " ", $cn ), 66 );

echo "\n\nNorway:\n";
$cn = DateTimeZone::listIdentifiers( DateTimeZone::PER_COUNTRY, "NO" );
echo wordwrap( join( " ", $cn ), 66 );
?>
```

When run, this script returns:

```
USA:
America/Adak America/Anchorage America/Boise America/Chicago
America/Denver America/Detroit America/Indiana/Indianapolis
America/Indiana/Knox America/Indiana/Marengo
America/Indiana/Petersburg America/Indiana/Tell_City
America/Indiana/Vevay America/Indiana/Vincennes
America/Indiana/Winamac America/Juneau America/Kentucky/Louisville
America/Kentucky/Monticello America/Los_Angeles America/Menominee
America/New_York America/Nome America/North_Dakota/Center
America/North_Dakota/New_Salem America/Phoenix America/Shiprock
America/Yakutat Pacific/Honolulu

China:
Asia/Chongqing Asia/Harbin Asia/Kashgar Asia/Shanghai Asia/Urumqi

Norway:
Europe/Oslo
```

As you can see from this example, both the US and China have multiple zones, where as Norway does not. From the example above, one other thing might draw some attention. While most countries' main timezone identifier is a match with the capital (such as Oslo), this is not the case for the US (Washington DC) or China (Beijing). The reason for this is that the Olson database where PHP obtains its data from uses the most populous city in a timezone as the name for that timezone. This is why the main timezone on the US east coast is America/New_York and in China Asia/Shanghai.

Chapter 4

Representing Date/Time Information

After you've obtained a time stamp with the `strtotime()` function, or a `DateTime` object with the `new DateTime` or `DateTime::createFromFormat()` methods that are described in the previous chapter, you most likely want to display it. For formatting timestamps, there are two functions to format the value as a string: `date()` and `strftime()`. There is another function to retrieve one of the associated elements as an integer: `idate()`. For formatting a `DateTime` object a different function is required. Both the procedural function `date_format()` and the OO method `DateTime->format()` allow you to format such an object.

Formatting Time Stamps

The `date()` function works relatively simply. As one of the arguments, you specify a format string. This format string describes which date/time values are going to be a part of the returned string, in which format, and in which order. The `date()` function also accepts an optional second argument—the time stamp. If this argument is not supplied, then the format string will be applied to the current date/time. Most often however, the second argument is supplied, as this specifies the Unix time stamp that is going to be formatted.

The format string contains "format specifiers" that control which information to display, and also additional characters. Each format specifier is either an uppercase or lowercase letter. Unrecognized format specifiers are copied to the output string as-is. If you want to use one of the format specifiers as a regular letter, you will have to escape it with the \ character. In some extreme cases you might have to escape the format specifier twice—when \ specifier already means something to PHP, like \t. For a full overview of all the supported format specifiers, see Appendix B. It might be a good idea to always escape letters, even if there is no format associated with a letter. The reason for this is that any letter can be assigned a format at a later date by the PHP developers.

So much for the theoretical background, let's have a look at some of the format specifiers. As an example we want to format the current time according to the standard American time format. This format consists of the parts in the following table.

Specifier	Description
g	hour—in 12-hour notation, without leading zero
i	minute—with leading zero
a	meridian (am or pm)

The two separators (colon and space) do not require a specific format specifier. The whole format string looks now like g:i a. The following code shows this format in action.

```php
<?php
echo date( 'g:i a' ), "\n";
?>
```

When run, this script returns:

```
9:55 pm
```

There are of course many other format specifiers, for all the different date/time elements. Besides the multitude of format specifiers for year, month, day, hour, minute and second, there are a few more special ones as well. See Appendix B for the full overview.

ISO Week Dates

The ISO 8601 standard includes a section that defines a different type of calendar based on Year-Week-DayOfWeek and defines an algorithm on how to number those three elements. The days of week are defined as 1 (Monday) to 7 (Sunday) and it states that every year has 52 or 53 weeks. Week 1 is the week with the first Thursday of the year, and the last week of the year (week 52 or 53) is the week with the year's last Thursday in it. This means that the natural year might be different from the ISO year for a few days. This scheme is often used in the fiscal world.

Let's take the last days of 2008 as an example. The definition states that the last week of the year is the week in which the last Thursday falls. For 2008 this is Thursday, December 25th. The next week (starting with Monday, December 28th) falls therefore in the new ISO year 2009 and has the week number one. This gives for December 29th to December 31th as ISO year "2009" while of course the natural year is still 2008. The corresponding ISO week date for Tuesday, December 30th, 2008 is "2009-W01-2"—year 2009, week 1 and day 2.

In order to display this ISO week date, you can of course not use the format specifier for the natural year (Y), but instead you have to use a different one for the ISO year, which is specifier o (lowercase O). This goes hand in hand with the specifier for the ISO week number W and the ISO day of week specifier N. Make sure to avoid the other day of week specifier w here, as this defines 0 as Sunday and 6 as Saturday.

To format the full date using the ISO week date scheme, you can either use o-\WW-N or the compact form o\WWN. Because of the compact form, the W specifier will use a leading zero if the week number consists of only one digit. Applying both formats to today's date, would return the following date strings:

```
Full: 2008-W19-3
Compact: 2008W193
```

There is a quick trick to find out how many ISO weeks a specific year has. Equivalent with the statement "The last week of the ISO year is the week which has the last Thursday of the year in it," is simply "The week with December 28th in it". Because of this, obtaining the number of weeks is fairly trivial as we can see in the following code.

```php
<?php
// uses the current year (2008 during the time of writing)
echo date( 'W', strtotime( "December 28th" ) ), "\n";
echo date( 'W', strtotime( "December 28th, 2009" ) ), "\n";
?>
```

When run this script shows:

```
52
53
```

Properties of Date/Time Elements

Some of the format specifiers are not necessarily meant to be used in a format string for displaying a specific date or time. Those specifiers can be used to obtain information about a specific date or time unit. For the year there is the L specifier, which returns a 1 in case the year is a leap year, or a 0 in case the year belonging to the date/time being formatted is not a leap year.[1]

The t specifier returns (as string) the number of days in the current month. It's value is either 28, 30 or 31 in normal years, or 29, 30 or 31 in leap years. Another special specifier, I (capital i), can be used to find out whether the current date is in daylight savings time or not. If it is, the specifier prints a 1, if it isn't, a 0.

Compound Formats

A few of the supported format specifiers return more information than one specific date/time element. These can be used instead of assembling an often used format yourself. There is r which formats according to RFC 2822 Internet Message Format. This is the format that is used in e-mail headers and looks like:

```
Wed, 07 May 2008 22:04:10 +0200
```

---

[1] Side note: In the Gregorian calendar the chance for a specific year to be a leap year is 24.25% and the chance for any specific day to be in a leap year is 24.30%.

Another supported format specifier for a compound format is c which will format the date/time string as a full ISO 8601 date, which looks like:

```
2008-05-07T22:05:47+02:00
```

Because the number of format specifiers is rather limited, there are no format specifiers for other compound formats. Instead there are a few constants that correspond to a format string containing the correct format specifiers for these formats. As these also have descriptive names, they are also much easier to remember than single format specifiers, or a specific group of format specifiers. The constants are both available as normal PHP constants, but also as class constants as part of the DateTime class. The class constants are listed in the following table. If you prefer to use a normal constant, replace DateTime:: in the Constant column with DATE_. To format a date for an e-mail header, you can use either of the methods as outlined in the following code.

```php
<?php
echo date( 'r' ), "\n";
echo date( DATE_RFC2822 ), "\n";
echo date( DateTime::RFC2822 ), "\n";
echo date( 'D, d M Y H:i:s O' ), "\n";
?>
```

Constant	Description	Example
DateTime::ATOM	Atom format (RFC 4287)	2005-05-08T21:52:01 +00:00
DateTime::COOKIE	HTTP Cookie Date Format (RFC 850)(The cookie specification requires the timezone to be GMT—the format will not handle that automatically for you. See Chapter 3 on how you can set the DateTime object's timezone to GMT.)	Monday, 08-May-05 21:52:01 UTC

DateTime::RSS	RSS 2.0, same as RFC 1123	Mon, 08 May 2008 21:52:01 +0000
DateTime::ISO8601	Full ISO 8601 format	2005-05-08T21:52:01+0000
DateTime::RFC822	Old e-mail headers standard	Mon, 08 May 05 21:52:01 +0000
DateTime::RFC850	Old Usenet date format (NNTP)	Monday, 08-May-05 21:52:01 UTC
DateTime::RFC1036	Updated Usenet date format (NNTP)	Mon, 08 May 05 21:52:01 +0000
DateTime::RFC1123	"Requirements for Internet Hosts"	Mon, 08 May 2005 21:52:01 +0000
DateTime::RFC2822	Updated e-mail standard	Mon, 08 May 2005 21:52:01 +0000
DateTime::RFC3339	The same as ATOM	2008-05-08T21:52:01+00:00

Local Time vs. UTC Time

The date() function always uses the current default timezone as configured through the date.timezone php.ini setting or the date_default_timezone_set() function. You can find information about the INI setting in Chapter 1 and information about the date_default_timezone_set() function in Chapter 3. In order to be able to format the HTTP Cookie format from the previous table correctly you need however to use the GMT timezone. The gmdate() function does just that. It ignores the default timezone and always formats the time stamp according to GMT. This means that all the format specifiers listed in Appendix B that deal with timezones behave different and will *always* use GMT and UTC-offset 0. Formatting a timestamp for use in a HTTP Cookie header is shown in the following code.

```php
<?php
echo gmdate( DateTime::COOKIE ), "\n";
?>
```

This script displays when executed:

```
Thursday, 08-May-08 20:33:03 GMT
```

You need to be aware however that when you're printing only a date, the result might be different from what you expect. For example, the following code will not show the "correct" date.

```php
<?php
echo gmdate( "Y-m-d", strtotime( "2008-05-10" ) ), "\n";
?>
```

This script displays when executed:

```
2008-05-09
```

This might look strange at first site, but it can be explained relatively easily. Because strtotime() returns a time stamp and not a DateTime object all information about time zones is lost. Because of this, gmdate() can not know anything about the context in which the date "2008-05-10" was parsed. This results in gmdate() printing a different date then what you expect. To see what really happened, you can simple print the whole date by using the DateTime::ISO8601 format. In that case the output would have been:

```
2008-05-09T22:00:00+0000
```

And that would have made the whole issue much clearer. To avoid this issue alto-gether it's wiser to use DateTime objects, or explicitly mention the UTC or GMT time zone abbreviation in the call to strtotime(): "2008-05-10 UTC".

Formatting Local Time Stamps

Up until now we've only seen English names for days and months. Unfortunately, there isn't any good way for localizing those names to whatever language you want. The only function capable of formatting according to a specific locale's rules and guidelines is with the strftime() function. This function uses the locale informa-tion as set through setlocale() function. A locale is a set of rules that define how a specific language/region combination prefers to see certain information. There are different categories, such as sorting rules (LC_COLLATE), character classifica-tion and conversion (LC_CTYPE), decimal separator (LC_NUMERIC) and of course date/time formatting (LC_TIME). The setlocale() function allows you to set a spe-cific locale for each of those categories (or all at one at the same time). However, the way to specify a locale depends on the Operating System. And even then, the Operating System might not even have the locales installed in the first place. Most Unix-like Operating Systems use the POSIX standard. POSIX uses locale names in the format ll_RR.C—where ll is the language code (following ISO 639-1), RR is the coun-try/region code (following ISO 3166-1 alpha-2) and C is the character set (for example UTF-8 or ISO-8859-1). An example of a full locale identifier is nb_NO.UTF-8 (Norwegian Bokmål, Norway, UTF-8). Windows however uses simple three letter identifiers fol-lowing ISO 3166-1 alpha-3, but also supports the English name of a country/region has locale identifier, and sometimes a random addition.[2] PHP's setlocale() func-tion allows you to provide it an array of locale identifiers to try, making it slightly easier to select a locale. The following code uses setlocale() with an array of locale identifiers in an attempt to set the locale category for date/time formatting to the Norwegian locale.

```php
<?php
```

---

[2]The list is quite limited on Windows, and it does not take into account dif-ferent localizations per country. You can find the supported list in MSDN at http://msdn.microsoft.com/en-us/library/cdax410z.aspxPHP.

```
$newLocale = setlocale(
    LC_TIME,
    array( 'nb_NO.UTF-8', 'no_NO', 'norwegian', 'nor' ) );
if ( $newLocale === false )
{
  echo "The locale is not available on this system.\n";
}
else
{
  echo "The locale identifier used is: ", $newLocale, ".\n";
}
?>
```

If one of the locales is installed, you will get an output like:

```
The locale identifier used is: nb_NO.UTF-8.
```

When the locale has been configured with the setlocale() function you can then use strftime() to format according to this locale. Unlike date(), the format specifiers are not just characters, but they are always prefixed by %. The format string to format a date according to ISO 8601 looks then like %Y-%m-%d %H:%M:%S. The example in the following code ties both parts together, and also demonstrates the use of different locales.

```
<?php
// select Norwegian
setlocale( LC_ALL, array( 'nb_NO.UTF-8', 'nb_NO', 'nor' ) );
echo strftime( '%A %e. %B %Y, %X' ), "\n";

// select Dutch
setlocale( LC_ALL, array( 'nl_NL.UTF-8', 'nl_NL', 'nld' ) );
echo strftime( '%A %e. %B %Y, %X' ), "\n";

// select English, UK
setlocale( LC_ALL, array( 'en_GB.UTF-8', 'en_GB', 'uk' ) );
echo strftime( '%A %e. %B %Y, %X' ), "\n";

// select English, US
setlocale( LC_ALL, array( 'en_US.UTF-8', 'en_US', 'usa' ) );
echo strftime( '%A %e. %B %Y, %X' ), "\n";
?>
```

This script displays when executed, if you have the correct locales installed, perhaps depending on the Operating System, something like:

```
søndag 11. mai 2008, kl. 16.36 +0200
zondag 11. mei 2008, 16:36:57
Sunday 11. May 2008, 16:36:57
Sunday 11. May 2008, 04:36:57 PM
```

From this example you can see one other feature that formatting with strftime() has to offer: preferred formats. The %X modifier in the previous example stands for "The preferred time representation for the current locale without the date." Besides the preferred time format, there is also a specifier for the preferred date format (%x) and the preferred date and time format (%c). The latter is used in the example in the following code. All the format specifiers that strftime() might accept, can also be found in Appendix B, in the column "strftime."

```php
<?php
// select Dutch
setlocale( LC_ALL, array( 'nl_NL.UTF-8', 'nl_NL', 'nld' ) );
echo strftime( '%c' ), "\n";

// select English, UK
setlocale( LC_ALL, array( 'en_GB.UTF-8', 'en_GB', 'uk' ) );
echo strftime( '%c' ), "\n";

// select English, US
setlocale( LC_ALL, array( 'en_US.UTF-8', 'en_US', 'usa' ) );
echo strftime( '%c' ), "\n";
?>
```

This script displays when executed, if you have the correct locales installed, perhaps depending on the Operating System, something like:

```
sø. 11. mai 2008 kl. 16.53 +0200
zo 11 mei 2008 16:53:17 CEST
Sun 11 May 2008 16:53:17 CEST
Sun 11 May 2008 04:53:17 PM CEST
```

The `strftime()` function is not implemented directly by PHP, but by the Operating Systems' system libraries. This causes problems in the way that not all format specifiers are available on every platform, or that they don't behave the same on every platform. On top of that, PHP's implementation only takes a time stamp and not a `DateTime` object. This, and the fact that `strftime()` uses the `TZ` environment variable, means that it is impossible to use `strftime()` to properly format dates if time zones get involved. It is therefore best to ignore this function.

Retrieving Specific Date/Time Elements

In some cases you might not want to format a whole date/time string, because you're only interested in for example retrieving the number of days in the current month. The `idate()` function provides such functionality. Instead of accepting a full format string, it only accepts one format specifier and it returns exactly one integer value. This makes the following two equivalent in most cases:

```
$value = idate( $formatSpecifier );
$value = (int) date( $formatSpecifier[0] );
```

Most of the format specifiers are the same as you can see in Appendix B, although in many cases the format specifier of the "leading zero" variant is picked over the one that just shows the number. In most, if not all cases, the `date()` function is just as capable as the `idate()` function. In the example in the `idate()` function is used to obtain the current UTC offset.

```
<?php
date_default_timezone_set( 'America/Chicago' );
echo idate( 'Z' ), "\n";

date_default_timezone_set( 'Europe/Oslo' );
echo idate( 'Z' ), "\n";
?>
```

This script displays when executed, something similar to:

```
-18000
```

```
7200
```

The returned values depend on whether Daylight Savings Time is in effect or not.

DateTime Object Formatting

Up to now we've only really formatted Unix timestamps. Unix timestamps can't store timezone information because they're just integer numbers, I've mentioned that a few times already. Some date/time strings contain fractions which are lost if this integer (whole number) Unix time stamp is used as well.

Of course is there also a function and method to format the date/time information that is stored in a DateTime object. This includes formatting of fractions, as well as more powerful timezone handling. The procedural function is called date_format() whereas the Object Oriented approach uses the format() method of the DateTime class. The format specifiers are the same ones that the date() function uses.

The following code will demonstrate how formatting the DateTime object instead of the time stamp makes the fractions work properly.

```php
<?php
$ts = strtotime( "22:55:01.19527" );
echo date( 'H:i:s.u', $ts ), "\n";

$d = new DateTime( "22:55:37.81252" );
echo $d->format( 'H:i:s.u' ), "\n";
?>
```

This script outputs the following:

```
22:55:01.000000
22:55:37.812520
```

The DateTime objects have associated timezone information, something else that Unix timestamps miss. The date() function will always use the current default time-zone for formatting a time stamp, but the date_format() function, and DateTime's format() method will use the timezone information that is associated with an object. This difference can be clearly seen in the following code.

```
<?php
date_default_timezone_set( 'America/Los_Angeles' );
$ts = strtotime( "2008-06-11 19:13:45 UTC" );
$dt = new DateTime( "2008-06-11 19:13:45 UTC" );

echo date( 'Y-m-d H:i:s e', $ts ), "\n";
echo $dt->format( 'Y-m-d H:i:s e' ), "\n";
?>
```

This script outputs the following:

```
2008-06-11 12:13:45 America/Los_Angeles
2008-06-11 19:13:45 UTC
```

The U format specifier is not useful while formatting Unix time stamps because it would simply return the passed time stamp as a string. However, this specifier does make sense in case DateTime objects are involved. Because a DateTime object supports a much larger range than Unix time stamps[3] the U format specifier allows you to obtain a time stamp that would otherwise not be possible due to limitations in PHP's integer type. The only drawback is that you get it as a string, and not as an integer. However, for storing this into a database, this should be good enough. The example in the following code demonstrates this.

```
<?php
$ts = strtotime( "2008-06-11 22:07:24" );
$dt = new DateTime( "2008-06-11 22:07:24" );

echo date( 'U', $ts ), "\n";
echo $dt->format( 'U' ), "\n\n";

$ts = strtotime( "2042-06-11 22:07:24" );
$dt = new DateTime( "2042-06-11 22:07:24" );

echo date( 'U', $ts ), "\n";
echo $dt->format( 'U' ), "\n";
?>
```

This script outputs the following on a 32-bit machine:

---

[3]This is only true for 32-bit machines.

```
1213214844
1213214844

0
2286133644
```

On a 64-bit machine, it outputs:

```
1213214844
1213214844

2286133644
2286133644
```

Please be aware that the `DateTime` object does not support a `__toString()` method. It would be virtually impossible to pick a format that's both accepted locally and informative enough to represent the date/time information properly.

Chapter 5

Date/Time Manipulation

Up to now, we have only dealt with "time information" for *one* specific point in time. It is of course quite likely that you would also like to manipulate the created DateTime objects. PHP's Date/Time support contains functionality to do just that—and even in multiple ways. This chapter deals with all the different ways you can manipulate DateTime objects.

Manipulation While Parsing

PHP's Date/Time parser has always supported "relative time," but its functionality has been extended first in PHP 5.1, and later in PHP 5.3. Relative time adds or subtracts time from either a specified point in time, or from the current time. An example of a relative time string is "+1 day." This statement alone, will return a time stamp exactly one day in the future while considering DST changes when used with the strtotime() or date_create() new DateTime() methods. The following code shows an example of a simple relative string, as well as a more complicated one.

```php
<?php
echo date_create( '+1 day' )->format( "c\n" );

$str = '2008-07-22 20:43:18 3 weeks ago +4 hour';
echo date_create( $str )->format( "c\n" );
?>
```

When run, this script returns (at the time of writing):

```
2008-07-23T21:04:07+02:00
2008-07-02T00:43:18+02:00
```

PHP is quite flexible with relative date/time strings, and supports a vast amount of different keywords and phrases. On top of that, it's better to let PHP do all the calculations instead of doing them yourselves.

An often common mistake is to think that each day is 24 * 3600 seconds as the following code illustrates.

```php
<?php
date_default_timezone_set( 'Europe/Oslo' );
echo date( 'Y-m-d', strtotime( '2008-10-26' ) + ( 24 * 3600 ) ), "\n";
echo date( 'Y-m-d', strtotime( '2008-10-26 +1 day' ) ), "\n";
echo date_create( '2008-10-26 +1 day' )->format( "Y-m-d\n" );
?>
```

When run, this script returns:

```
2008-10-26
2008-10-27
2008-10-27
```

What happens here, is that the timezone Europe/Oslo switches from Daylight Savings Time back to normal time on exactly this date. This makes October 26th "25" hours long. The home-brewn calculation of 24 * 3600 will therefore be an hour short, and still show 2008-10-26. In the second and third lines this is not an issue as PHP's date/time support correctly accounts for DST transitions. I could show you many other cases like this, but it is better to focus on how it "should" be done.

We've already seen that you modify the date while parsing, by using one of the relative time statements with strtotime() and date_create(). Of course this is also supported when creating a new DateTime object with new DateTime(). strtotime() also allows you to modify an already existing time stamp by passing the time stamp as second argument to the function, and then use relative time exclusively as first argument.

Modifying an Existing DateTime Object

DateTime objects can also be modified outside of the constructor. There are a few different ways of modifying a DateTime object, which we'll describe in this section. Please note that from the methods below, the interval and iterator functionality is only supported in PHP 5.3 and later.

Setter Methods

The DateTime class contains a few setter methods to modify date/time information. These methods are setTime(), setDate(), setISODate() and setTimestamp(). Procedural versions of those methods are available as date_time_set(), date_date_set(), date_isodate_set() and date_timestamp_set().

The first of them—DateTime->setTime()—allows you to modify the time element of the date that is stored in the object. The method requires two arguments—one to set the new hour, and one to set the new minute. An optional third element allows you to specify seconds as well, and defaults to 0 in case it is not given. The following code example demonstrates this.

```php
<?php
$d = new DateTime( "2008-07-27 16:58:12" );
echo $d->format( "Y-m-d H:i:s\n" );

$d->setTime( 15, 8 );
echo $d->format( "Y-m-d H:i:s\n" );

$d->setTime( 17, 6, 31 );
echo $d->format( "Y-m-d H:i:s\n" );
?>
```

When run, this script returns:

```
2008-07-27 16:58:12
2008-07-27 15:08:00
2008-07-27 17:06:31
```

The second setter method is DateTime->setDate(). As the name describes, this method will modify the date part of the object. All of its three parameters (year, month and day) are required. The example in the following code demonstrates the use of this function and what happens when you provide a number that is either too low, or too high for a specific field.

```php
<?php
$d = new DateTime( "2008-07-27" );
echo $d->format( "Y-m-d\n" );

$d->setDate( 2008, 8, 8 );
echo $d->format( "Y-m-d\n" );

// underflow in day argument
$d->setDate( 2008, 9, 0 );
echo $d->format( "Y-m-d\n" );

// overflow in day argument
$d->setDate( 2008, 1, 276 );
echo $d->format( "Y-m-d\n" );
?>
```

When run, this script returns:

```
2008-07-27
2008-08-08
2008-08-31
2008-10-02
```

In the first setDate() call we simply set the date to August 8th, 2008. In the second call however, we underflow the day value by using 0. As there is no August 0th, the method interprets this as the last day of July—the 31st. In the last setDate() call we set the day to January 276th, 2008, which basically means the 276th day in the year. However, this can be done better with relative date/time strings as we will show later on.

Slightly related to the setDate() method is the setISODate() method. This one modifies the date on the DateTime object according to ISO 8601 week-day rules as explained in Chapter 4. This method requires two arguments, the year and the ISO week number. The third optional argument specifies the day-of-week, and defaults to 1 (Monday). The example in the following code demonstrates the use of this method.

```php
<?php
$d = new DateTime( "2008-07-27" );
echo $d->format( "Y-m-d\n" );

$d->setISODate( 2008, 32, 5 );
echo $d->format( "Y-m-d\n" );

$d->setISODate( 2008, 1, 1 );
echo $d->format( "Y-m-d\n" );

$d->setISODate( 2009, 53, 2 );
echo $d->format( "Y-m-d\n" );
?>
```

When run, this script returns:

```
2008-07-27
2008-08-08
2007-12-31
2009-12-29
```

As you can see this example, the first week of the year, can actually generate dates in the previous year (2007-12-31).

The last of the setter methods is setTimestamp(), and was introduced in PHP 5.3. This method allows you to re-create the DateTime object from a Unix time stamp. The following code demonstrates the use of setTimestamp().

```php
<?php
// construct a DateTime with a pre-set date and modify time stamp
$d = new DateTime( "2008-07-27" );
$d->setTimestamp( 1227184864 );
echo $d->format( "Y-m-d\n" );

// create a DateTime object from a time stamp
$d = new DateTime( '@1227184864' );
echo $d->format( "Y-m-d H:i e\n" );

// create a DateTime representing now, and them modify the time stamp
$d = new DateTime();
$d->setTimestamp( 1227184864 );
echo $d->format( "Y-m-d H:i e\n" );
?>
```

When run, this script returns:

```
2008-11-20
2008-11-20 12:41 +00:00
2008-11-20 13:41 Europe/Oslo
```

From this example we can also see that using setTimestamp() behaves differently than passing a time stamp directly in the constructor as we can see in line 8. If you pass a time stamp to a constructor, the timezone is always set to UTC. The current timezone is *not* affected when a new date/time is configured by calling setTimestamp() as you can see in lines 12 to 15 of the code, and the third line in the output.

Relative Strings

We already covered relative time strings while parsing a date/time string. PHP also allows you to use the same relative phrases after a DateTime object has already been created. The modify() method on the DateTime object (or the procedural equivalent date_modify()) accepts the same date/time strings as new DateTime() and date_create(). But instead of using the whole string, only the parts that are linked to relative time are used. In the following code, we use the modify() method to alter an already existing DateTime object.

```php
<?php
$d = new DateTime( "2008-07-29 21:35:47" );
echo $d->format( "l c\n" );

echo $d->modify( "+3 days" )->format( "l c\n" );

echo $d->modify( "next weekday" )->format( "l c\n" );

echo date_create( "2008-01-01" )
    ->modify( "+275 days" )
    ->setTimezone( new DateTimeZone( 'UTC' ) )
    ->format( "l c\n" );
?>
```

When run, this script returns:

```
Tuesday 2008-07-29T21:35:47+02:00
Friday 2008-08-01T21:35:47+02:00
Monday 2008-08-04T21:35:47+02:00
Wednesday 2008-10-01T22:00:00+00:00
```

Besides showing how modify() works, this example also demonstrates the chaining of method calls. Since PHP 5.3, all the methods of the DateTime object that only modify the object (such as the setters from the previous section, the modify(), add() and sub() methods) can be chained like this. In line 9 you see how we use date_create() instead of new DateTime() to circumvent PHP's restriction of not allowing method calls directly from new DateTime() as in new DateTime()->format(). In PHP 5.1 and 5.2, you will need to call each method separately on the object.

Intervals

An interval is basically the same as a relative date/time string as we've seen earlier in this chapter, except that it is in the form of an object with the class name DateInterval. This functionality is only available in PHP 5.3 and later.

Objects of this class can be created in different ways. The first one is through the class' constructor. new DateInterval() expects interval specifications according to ISO 8601 as parameter. There are three different formats for describing an ISO 8601 interval. The first format is PYYYY-MM-DDThh:mm:ss and describes an interval just like a normal date/time string except that it starts with a P (for period). P0003-01-15T06:12:30 stands for an interval of 3 years, 1 month, 15 days, 6 hours, 12 minutes and 30 seconds.

The second format is PnYnMnDTnHnMnS where each of the elements is allowed to be left out as long as it does not cause ambiguities. That means that "3 months" should be encoded as P3M, while "3 minutes" should be encoded as PT3M. If any of the time elements is present, the T is required to appear before them. The numbers itself are limited in PHP to 9 digits. The duration from the previous paragraph can be expressed as P3Y1M15DT6H12M30S.

In some cases you would want to represent the duration in years, weeks and days rather then in years, months and days. The third alternative format is therefore PnYnWnDTnHnMnS. The duration from the previous two paragraphs can then be encoded as P3Y6W4DT6H12M30D, but also as P3Y6W3DT... depending on context—a month could have either 30 or 31 days (or of course 28 or 29 for February). Alternatively you could use the duration P1142DT... to specify the duration in days instead.

The examples in the following code demonstrate how you can you use the constructor to initialize a DateInterval object.

```php
<?php
// full notation
$i = new DateInterval( 'P0003-01-15T06:12:30' );

// abbreviated notation
$i = new DateInterval( 'P3DT6H' );
$i = new DateInterval( 'PT23H56M04S' );

// approximate equivalents for one sidereal year
$i = new DateInterval( 'P365DT6H9M' );
$i = new DateInterval( 'P52W1DT6H9M' );
?>
```

The ISO 8601 interval strings are a bit limiting, as they only really support trivial differences with years, month, days, hours, minutes and seconds. The second method of creating a DateInterval object adds support for all the other relative time functionality that PHP supports. The DateInterval::createFromDateString() factory method (or the procedural variant date_interval_create_from_date_string()) provides this functionality.

This factory method accepts the same string as the DateTime->modify() method accepts. Instead of applying the string directly to the DateTime object it creates a DateInterval object that can be applied multiple times to a date object with the DateTime->add() method. The following shows two equivalent pieces of code.

```php
<?php
// Directly modifying the DateTime object
$d = new DateTime( "2008-08-02 17:43:02" );
$d->modify( "next weekday" );
echo $d->format( "l Y-m-d H:i:s\n" );

// With a simple date/time string
$d = new DateTime( "2008-08-02 17:43:02" );
$i = DateInterval::createFromDateString( "+42 days" );
$d->add( $i );
echo $d->format( "l Y-m-d H:i:s\n" );
```

```
// With a "special" date/time string
$i = DateInterval::createFromDateString( "next weekday" );
echo $d->add( $i )->format( "l Y-m-d H:i:s\n" );
echo $d->add( $i )->format( "l Y-m-d H:i:s\n" );
?>
```

When run, this scripts displays:

```
Monday 2008-08-04 17:43:02
Saturday 2008-09-13 17:43:02
Monday 2008-09-15 17:43:02
Tuesday 2008-09-16 17:43:02
```

The last way of creating a `DateInterval` object is by using the `DateTime->diff()` method (or `date_diff()`). This method is called on a `DateTime` object with as its sole argument another `DateTime` object. It compares those two objects and creates a `DateInterval` object describing the differences between the first and the second `DateTime` object. The obtained `DateInterval` object can then be used with the `DateTime->add()` or `DateTime->sub()` methods. You can not use the `DateTime->sub()` method with `DateInterval` objects that were created with the `DateInterval::createFromDateString()` method as it's virtually impossible to calculate the opposite version of some of the advanced relative date/time strings. The following code shows how to create a `DateInterval` object with the `DateTime->diff()` method.

```
<?php
$d1 = new DateTime( "2008-08-03" );
$d2 = new DateTime( "2008-08-08" );
// Calculates the difference (5 days)
$i = $d1->diff( $d2 );
// Add those 5 days to $d1
echo $d1->add( $i )->format( "l c\n" );
// Subtract those 5 days from $d2
echo $d2->sub( $i )->format( "l c\n" );
?>
```

When run, this scripts displays:

```
Friday 2008-08-08T00:00:00+02:00
Sunday 2008-08-03T00:00:00+02:00
```

If the second date—the one passed as argument to the `DateTime->diff()` method—describes a point in time before the `DateTime` object we call the method on, the `DateInterval` object will contain a negative interval. The example in the following code illustrates this.

```php
<?php
$d1 = new DateTime( "2008-08-08" );
$d2 = new DateTime( "2008-08-03" );
// Calculates the difference (-5 days)
$i = $d1->diff( $d2 );
// Add those -5 days to $d1
echo $d1->add( $i )->format( "l c\n" );
// Subtract those -5 days from $d2
echo $d2->sub( $i )->format( "l c\n" );
?>
```

When run, this scripts displays:

```
Sunday 2008-08-03T00:00:00+02:00
Friday 2008-08-08T00:00:00+02:00
```

Please be aware that using `DateInterval` objects created with the `DateInterval::createFromDateString()` method with `DateTime->sub()` might not work as you expect. The `DateTime->sub()` method only works with "simple" intervals that only deal with the year, month, day, hour, minute and second primitives.

Those primitives are all accessible through properties of the `DateInterval` object as the following code shows.

```php
<?php
$d1 = new DateTime( "1978-12-22 09:15" );
$d2 = new DateTime( "now" );
$i = $d1->diff( $d2 );

echo "{$i->y} years, {$i->m} months, {$i->d} days, ".
     "{$i->h} hours, {$i->i} minutes and {$i->s} seconds.\n";
```

```
?>
```

When run, this scripts displays (at the time of writing):

```
29 years, 7 months, 12 days, 4 hours, 44 minutes and 49 seconds.
```

Besides the properties shown in the previous example, there is also a property `invert`. When this value of this property is 1, the `DateTime` object that was passed as argument to the `DateTime->diff()` method described a point in time before the object that the method was called on. The other property is `days`—which contains the total number of days between the two dates. This property is useful to find out the exact number of days between two dates, as the years/months/days combination from earlier is not representative of this. A year could have 365 or 366 days, while a month could have 28-31 days.

The `DateInterval->format()` method also allows you to obtain information from a `DateInterval` object. The format specifiers are documented in Appendix B, but an example can be seen in the following code.

```php
<?php
$d1 = new DateTime( "1978-12-22 09:15" );
$d2 = new DateTime( "now" );
$i = $d1->diff( $d2 );
echo $i->format( "%R%y yrs, %m mnths, %d days (%a days), ".
  "%h hrs, %i mins and %s secs.\n" );

$d2 = new DateTime( "2008-08-03 15:10" );
$d1 = new DateTime( "2008-12-22" );
$i = $d1->diff( $d2 );

echo $i->format( "%R%y yrs, %m mnths, %d days (%a days), ".
  "%h hrs, %i mins and %s secs.\n" );
?>
```

When run, this scripts displays (at the time of writing):

```
+29 yrs, 7 mnths, 12 days (10817 days), 5 hrs, 56 mins and 54 secs.
-0 yrs, 4 mnths, 18 days (140 days), 8 hrs, 50 mins and 0 secs.
```

Periods and Iterators

Sometimes it is useful to list all dates in a specific range, perhaps with custom intervals. Since PHP 5.3, PHP supports periods (re-occurrences of intervals) with the `DatePeriod` class. The constructor of the `DatePeriod` class accepts arguments in three distinct ways. The first two both accept a starting `DateTime` object and an interval in the form of a `DateInterval` object. They differ however with how the end time is determined. With the first method, the number of occurrences is simply passed as we can see in the following code.

```php
<?php
$db = new DateTime( '2008-07-31' );
$di = DateInterval::createFromDateString( 'next weekday' );

foreach ( new DatePeriod( $db, $di, 3 ) as $dt )
{
  echo $dt->format( "l Y-m-d\n" );
}
?>
```

When run, this scripts displays:

```
Thursday 2008-07-31
Friday 2008-08-01
Monday 2008-08-04
Tuesday 2008-08-05
```

The second method you pass the end date in the form of a `DateTime` object. The following code demonstrates this.

```php
<?php
$db = new DateTime( '2008-07-31' );
$de = new DateTime( '2008-08-05' );
$di = DateInterval::createFromDateString( 'next weekday' );

foreach ( new DatePeriod( $db, $di, $de ) as $dt )
{
  echo $dt->format( "l Y-m-d\n" );
}
?>
```

When run, this scripts displays:

```
Thursday 2008-07-31
Friday 2008-08-01
Monday 2008-08-04
```

The third method uses a totally different approach and obtains the start, end and interval information from something that resembles an ISO 8601 interval string. The string is required to have a start date (in full ISO 8601 format), an interval (in ISO 8601 P notation) and either an end date (in full ISO 8601 format) or the number of repetitions in the form Rn. Each of those three elements needs to be separated by a / and the order is irrelevant except for that the start date is the first date encountered, and the end date always the second (if available). The following code shows two examples on how to use DatePeriod() with a string.

```php
<?php
$s = 'R3/2008-08-04T20:21:35Z/P2D';
foreach ( new DatePeriod( $s ) as $dt )
{
  echo $dt->format( "l Y-m-d\n" );
}
echo "\n";

$s = "2008-10-04T20:56:18Z/P0000-00-20T03:15:54/2008-12-22T00:00:00Z";
foreach ( new DatePeriod( $s ) as $dt )
{
  echo $dt->format( "Y-m-d H:i:s\n" );
}
?>
```

In the first one we specify the number of recurrences with R3, the start date with 2008-08-04T20:21:35Z and the interval with P2D. In the second one we specify the start date with 2008-10-04T20:56:18Z the interval with P0000-00-20T03:15:54 and the end date with 2008-12-22T00:00:00Z. When run, this script displays:

```
Monday 2008-08-04
Wednesday 2008-08-06
Friday 2008-08-08
Sunday 2008-08-10
```

```
2008-10-04 20:56:18
2008-10-25 00:12:12
2008-11-14 03:28:06
2008-12-04 06:44:00
```

Be aware that by default, the start date will be returned as the first DateTime object from the iterator. If you do not want that, you can use as an additional argument the option DatePeriod::EXCLUDE_START_DATE like in the following code.

```php
<?php
$s = 'R3/2008-08-04T20:21:35Z/P2D';
foreach ( new DatePeriod( $s, DatePeriod::EXCLUDE_START_DATE ) as $dt )
{
  echo $dt->format( "l Y-m-d\n" );
}
echo "\n";
?>
```

Also note that the start and end dates in ISO 8601 format are required to have a Z at the end. This Z means that UTC is being used. The ISO 8601 interval format also allows you to remove every insignificant part, such as only specifying a date (2008-08-04). PHP does not support this at the moment and requires the full format to be used. This is also true for the long interval format PYYYY-MM-DDTHH:II:SS. PHP requires the full format here as well. If you do not want to be restricted to using UTC for the start and end date, you can use the DatePeriod construct that accepts date objects instead.

Chapter 6

Practical Date/Time Handling

This chapter contains a number of practical guidelines on how to perform a number of often occurring tasks.

Timezones

Finding the Next DST Transition

The DateTimeZone->getTransitions() method can be used to find out when the next change from/to Daylight Savings Time occurs. To do so, we basically have to loop over the array returned by the getTransitions() method and find out what the first transition after the current time is. This is what the example in following code does.

```php
<?php
$tz = new DateTimeZone( 'Europe/Oslo' );
$transitions = $tz->getTransitions( time(), strtotime( '+1 year' ) );

$nextTr = $transitions[1];
$time = $nextTr['ts'] - 1;

$d = new DateTime( "@{$time}" );
$d->setTimeZone( $tz );

printf( "The timezone %s switches to %s on:\n\t%s\n",
  $tz->getName(),
```

```
    $nextTr['isdst'] ? "DST" : "standard time",
    $d->format( 'Y-m-d @ H:i:s T' ) );
printf( "The new GMT offset will be:\n\t%d (%s)\n",
    $nextTr['offset'], $nextTr['abbr'] );
?>
```

When run, this script returns something similar to:

```
The timezone Europe/Oslo switches to standard time on:
  2008-10-26 @ 02:59:59 CEST
The new GMT offset will be:
  3600 (CET)
```

In line 3 we fetch the transitions from the current time until next year. This only works in PHP 5.3 and later. In case you want to use this code with PHP 5.2, replace lines 3-5 with:

```
foreach ( $transitions as $nextTr )
{
  if ( $nextTr['ts'] > time() )
  {
    break;
  }
}
```

Also note that in line 9 we set the timezone of the newly created DateTime object to the timezone that we're working with. This is required because by default, all DateTime objects that are created from a Unix time stamp, have the timezone UTC associated as described in Chapter 2.

Guessing from the Browser

Often you're not really interested in the timezone that the server has, but instead you want to format a date time according to the timezone in which the viewer of your website is. The only real way by doing that is through client-side JavaScript. Unfortunately, JavaScript's date/time handling is not nearly up to par with PHP, and only allows you to retrieve the UTC offset and a date/time formatted according to the current locale. In some cases, this locale formatted string contains the timezone abbreviation. In the following code, we'll try to fetch that information, and use it to find the user's timezone.

```php
<?php
if (!isset($_GET['tzinfo'])) {
?>
<html>
<script type="text/javascript">
var d = new Date()
var tzo = d.getTimezoneOffset()
var tza = d.toLocaleString().split(" ").slice(-1)
window.location = window.location + '?tzinfo=' + tza + '|' + tzo
</script>
</html>
<?php
} else {
    list( $abbr, $offset ) = explode( '|', $_GET['tzinfo'] );
    echo timezone_name_from_abbr( $abbr, $offset * -60 );
}
?>
```

This script works by making two requests. In the first request a form is shown (lines 4-11) that uses JavaScript to get some of the date/time parameters. In line 7 we use the getTimezoneOffset() method of the Date object to find the current UTC offset. Line 8 formats this Date object according to the current locale. For this script to work, we expect that the last part of this string contains a timezone abbreviation such as CEST. Whether this is actually the case greatly depends on browser, installed locale and location.

With those two obtained details, we then re-request the script in line 9 - but with the details appended to the URL ('?tzinfo=' + tza + '|' + tzo). This information is extracted from the URL in line 14. With the timezone abbreviation in $abbr and the UTC offset in $offset we then call the timezone_name_from_abbr() function with those parameters. This function tries to find a timezone identifier from the passed abbreviation. It can do this with just the abbreviation, but it is much more accurate if more information is provided. The optional 2nd argument expects the UTC-offset in seconds and the optional 3rd argument whether DST is in effect or not. This makes:

```php
echo timezone_name_from_abbr( "est" ), "\n";
```

show `America/New_York`, but:

```
echo timezone_name_from_abbr( "est", 36000 ), "\n";
```

show `Australia/ACT`. Unfortunately, this function can not be 100% correct because abbreviations are not unique, but with the additional UTC offsets and whether DST is in effect it is pretty accurate. If only JavaScript would provide that information life would be much easier. As a conclusion, the `timezone_name_from_abbr()` can be useful to guess the user's timezone, but you should always allow the possibility for the user to change this setting.

Date-Only Applications

In some cases your PHP application might only have to deal with dates, and times are not important. In this cases, timezones only complicate matters, and therefore you might consider to set your timezone setting to simply `UTC`. This also speeds up calculations, as no timezone guessing algorithms have to run.

With the timezone set to `UTC` you could even get away by calculating the difference between two dates by simply dividing the number of seconds by 86400. Of course, you should be using real `DateTime` objects and in this case using `date_diff()` is preferred.

Storing Date/Time Information in a Database

There are basically two major methods of storing date/time information in databases. The first one is by the use of Unix timestamps, and the second one is by using database provided data types. The main difference between those two methods is, that if you store timestamps in integer columns yourself, you have full control over timezone conversions, but if you use the database's date/time data types you leave timezone conversions to the database.

MySQL

MySQL's support for timezones is rather limited, and does not allow you to input any timezone information while inserting a value into a date/time column (both

DATETIME and TIMESTAMP data-types). Timezone support in MySQL allows you to specify the timezone in three different ways. First of all, MySQL will use the system's timezone information. You can change the server timezone by starting the server with the −−timezone=timezone_name option, or by setting the TZ environment variable. The timezone_name is a system specific timezone name, which makes support for this depend on the Operating System. The second way to set a timezone is by changing the global system time. The global system timezone defaults to SYSTEM—the system's timezone, but can be changed by either passing the −−default-time-zone option while starting the server, setting the default-time-zone option in an option file, or by issuing as a user with SUPER privileges:

```
SET GLOBAL time_zone = timezone;
```

The last method for setting a timezone, is by setting the per-connection timezone with the statement:

```
SET time_zone = timezone;
```

This will set the timezone for the current connection only. To what the current timezone settings are set to, you can use:

```
SELECT @@global.time_zone, @@session.time_zone;
```

The timezone value in the above paragraph can have different kinds of values. SYSTEM means that the timezone is used as the Operating System sees it. A value of +10:00 or -04:30 means that a specific UTC offset is used for conversions. MySQL also supports the timezones from the Olsen database, however in order to use those you would need to do some work.

To make the Olsen timezone database available, you need to use the mysql_tzinfo_to_sql program. This program takes a directory with timezone files (usually /usr/share/zoneinfo) and loads that into MySQL's mysql database. The tables for this should already have been created when MySQL was installed, but they are empty by default. In most situations, running the command following command on the shell will load the timezone information:

```
mysql_tzinfo_to_sql /usr/share/zoneinfo | mysql -u root mysql
```

You will need to do this every time that the Olsen timezone database gets updated in order to keep the data up-to-date. See the MySQL manual at http://dev.mysql.com/doc/refman/5.1/en/mysql-tzinfo-to-sql.html for more detailed instructions. The system database might be out of sync with PHP, so it is actually a good idea to rewrite the mysql_tzinfo_to_sql program in PHP. Instead of the system timezone you can then use PHP's built-in timezone database. The following script does exactly this.

```php
<?php
echo <<<ENDE
TRUNCATE TABLE time_zone;
TRUNCATE TABLE time_zone_name;
TRUNCATE TABLE time_zone_transition;
TRUNCATE TABLE time_zone_transition_type;

ENDE;
$tzs = timezone_identifiers_list();

foreach( $tzs as $tzName )
{
  echo "INSERT INTO time_zone(Use_leap_seconds) VALUES ('N');\n";
  echo "SET @time_zone_id= LAST_INSERT_ID();\n";
  echo "INSERT INTO time_zone_name (Name, Time_zone_id) VALUES ('$tzName',
      @time_zone_id);\n";

  $first = true;
  $tzObj = new DateTimeZone( $tzName );
  $transitions = $tzObj->getTransitions();

  $types = array();
  foreach ( $transitions as $tr )
  {
    $key = "{$tr['offset']}|{$tr['isdst']}|{$tr['abbr']}";
    if ( !in_array( $key, $types ) )
    {
      $types[] = $key;
    }
    if (-PHP_INT_MAX-1 == $tr['ts'] )
    {
      continue;
```

```php
  }
  $typeId = array_search( $key, $types );

  if ( $first )
  {
    echo "INSERT INTO time_zone_transition (Time_zone_id, Transition_time,
        Transition_type_id) VALUES\n";
    echo " ";
    $first = false;
  }
  else
  {
    echo ",";
  }
  echo "(@time_zone_id, {$tr['ts']}, {$typeId})\n";
}
if ( !$first )
{
  echo ";\n";
}

$first = true;
echo "INSERT INTO time_zone_transition_type (Time_zone_id, Transition_type_id,
    Offset, Is_DST, Abbreviation) VALUES\n";
foreach ( $types as $key => $type )
{
  list( $offset, $isdst, $abbr ) = explode( "|", $type );
  if ( $first )
  {
    echo " ";
    $first = false;
  }
  else
  {
    echo ",";
  }
  $isdst = $isdst ? '1' : '0';
  echo "(@time_zone_id, {$key}, {$offset}, {$isdst}, '{$abbr}')\n";
}
echo ";\n";

}
?>
```

The script should be run every time the timezone database is updated—which in PHP can happen by an upgrade to a newer PHP version, or when you've installed a new version of the timezone database as described in Appendix A.

Please note that the timezone settings only have effect on TIMESTAMP columns, and not on DATETIME, DATE and TIME columns. The functions NOW() and CURTIME() also use the timezone settings, as well as their synonyms CURRENT_TIMESTAMP() and CURRENT_TIME().

The following sequence shows some of the above mentioned functionality:

```
mysql> create table tz_test( dt datetime, ts timestamp );
Query OK, 0 rows affected (0.02 sec)

mysql> set time_zone = 'Europe/Berlin';
Query OK, 0 rows affected (0.00 sec)

mysql> insert into tz_test values( '2008-01-08 18:55', '2008-01-08 18:15' );
Query OK, 1 row affected (0.00 sec)

mysql> insert into tz_test values( '2008-09-08 18:55', '2008-09-08 18:15' );
Query OK, 1 row affected (0.00 sec)

mysql> select * from tz_test;
+---------------------+---------------------+
| dt                  | ts                  |
+---------------------+---------------------+
| 2008-01-08 18:55:00 | 2008-01-08 18:15:00 |
| 2008-09-08 18:55:00 | 2008-09-08 18:15:00 |
+---------------------+---------------------+
2 rows in set (0.00 sec)

mysql> set time_zone = '+00:00';
Query OK, 0 rows affected (0.00 sec)

mysql> select * from tz_test;
+---------------------+---------------------+
| dt                  | ts                  |
+---------------------+---------------------+
| 2008-01-08 18:55:00 | 2008-01-08 17:15:00 |
| 2008-09-08 18:55:00 | 2008-09-08 16:15:00 |
+---------------------+---------------------+
2 rows in set (0.00 sec)
```

The last select shows that DATETIME columns are not affected by timezones and always return the same value no matter what, while TIMESTAMP columns change the value according to the timezone settings. In this case the two times are off because one was during Daylight Savings Time, while the other one was not. MySQL does not allow you to specify any timezone when inserting a date/time value into a TIMESTAMP column, it will always use the current timezone.

PostgreSQL

PostgreSQL's support for timezones is quite a bit better, but only in the more recent versions (since 8.2). Unlike MySQL, PostgreSQL does allow you to specify a timezone while inserting a value into a TIMESTAMP WITH TIME ZONE or TIME WITH TIMEZONE column. Timezones can be specified as a UTC offset (-8, -08:00) directly behind a time string such as in 04:05:06-08:00 or 20:51:18+8, as a timezone abbreviation such as CEST in 20:52 CEST, or as timezone identifier such as Europe/Oslo in 2008-10-03 20:53:17 Europe/Oslo. If you use a timezone identifier, then the date *has* to be present—even if you're inserting into a TIME WITH TIME ZONE column which does not record the date. This is required because the date determines whether DST is in effect or not. The PostgreSQL manual recommends to not use the TIME WITH TIME ZONE column type. Timezones are ignored in columns that do not have WITH TIME ZONE as part of their column definitions. The database always stores timestamps in UTC time. If no timezone has been specified the *current timezone* is used.

The *current timezone* is determined by PostgreSQL in a way that very much resembles PHP's methods. First of all, PostgreSQL can be configured with a runtime parameter called timezone. This setting can be either made in postgresql.conf or on the command line when starting the server. In case the setting is not present, PostgreSQL checks the TZ environment variable. If this environment variable is not defined, or if it contains a timezone name that PostgreSQL does not recognize it attempts to guess the timezone by using the system's localtime() functionality. It then chooses the closest match compared to the database's list of timezone information.

All of the above determines the server timezone, however, the timezone can also be set on the client side. With the SQL command SET TIME ZONE you can set the timezone for the current session (connection). This command accepts several different kind of values. You can set it to a timezone identifier, like in SET TIME ZONE

'Europe/Oslo';; to a timezone abbreviation; to a UTC offset, like in SET TIME ZONE -7;; or to LOCAL (in which case the server's timezone is used). If you set the PGTZ environment variable on the client side, a SET TIME ZONE SQL command will automatically be run with the value of the PGTZ environment variable.

PostgreSQL allows you to configure how timezone abbreviations map by making certain server configurations, please see http://www.postgresql.org/docs/8.2/static/datetime-config-files.html. The manual also explains how PostgreSQL parses and deals with date time input at http://www.postgresql.org/docs/8.3/static/datetime-appendix.html. Unlike MySQL, it does not seem to be possible to configure which timezone rules PostgreSQL uses.

Timestamps

As an alternative to relying on the databases to deal with timezone conversions, you can also resort to taking care of things yourself. Instead of using the Databases' date/time specific columns you can chose to store all date/time information in an integer column as a Unix time stamp. This has the disadvantage that you have to do the conversion from DateTime object to a Unix time stamp yourself with PHP. Advantages however are that there are no discrepancies between the timezone information in PHP and the RDBMS and that using Unix time stamps is fully RDBMS independent. However, we've mentioned before that a time stamp alone does not allow you to construct a proper DateTime object that correctly transitions between timezone rules. For this, you would also need to record the timezone identifier to go with a time stamp. This is of course only important if you want to be able to reconstruct the original object.

To store a DateTime object in a database, you'd need to define two fields: a signed integer column to store the time stamp, and a char column to store the timezone identifier. You can then use something like the following code to create the values for the two columns:

```php
<?php
list( $timestamp, $timezoneIdentifier ) =
    explode( ' ', $dateObj->format( 'U e') );
?>
```

After reading the time stamp and timezone identifier back from the database, you can re-create the object with the following code:

```php
<?php
$dateObj = new DateTime( "@$timestamp" );
$dateObj->setTimezone( new DateTimeZone( $timezoneIdentifier ) );
?>
```

Manipulating Date/Time Objects

Appendix C describes all the relative time formats that the parser understands. But we will continue with some practical examples.

Previous Week Information

Obtaining the Monday and Friday of previous week requires a little bit of thinking. You might be inclined to think that "last Monday" means "the Monday of the previous week"—however, that is not true. If today's day is not a Monday, but for example a Thursday, then "last Monday" would represent the Monday *directly* before this Thursday. Last week's Monday could be represented by -1 week last monday. However, if today's day is a Monday, then -1 week last monday would represent a Monday *two weeks* ago. Now, to understand this behavior, we need to dive a bit more into how the parser works.

In the above text there are a few distinct phrases that the parser understands. Those are -1 week, monday, last monday and ago. Each of those phrases has a specific meaning to the parser. The first one (-1 week) sets the relative day count to 7 times the number of weeks (-1 in our example). -1 week will therefore set the day count to -7.

The second phrase (monday) sets the relative day number to the day of the week (0 for Sunday, 1 for Monday through 6 for Saturday). Because the day name is standalone, the *behavior modifier* is set to 1. This behavior modifier determines what should happen if the parser encounters a day name. Sometimes a date string resembles something like Sunday April 20th, 2008. In this case, the day name Sunday is parsed but it should not have any influence on the matching time stamp as April

20th, 2008 is a Sunday. However, the name of the day in the date string Monday April 20th, 2008 does have a meaning, as April 20th is not a Sunday. In this case the text Monday makes the date advance the first Monday after the parsed date. The phrase this Sunday has the same meaning to the parser as Sunday and therefore this Sunday April 20th, 2008 as the same meaning as Sunday April 20th, 2008. The other behavior (0) is when an encountered day name *does* influence the behavior of the matching time stamp.

The third phrase (last monday) is an example of this. When a modifier (such as next, last, second etc.) is used, the other behavior is activated. Please be aware that the this keyword does *not* switch to this behavior. The phrase this Sunday has therefore the same meaning to the parser as Sunday.

The last phrase (ago) tells the parser to invert *all* elements that have a non-zero value that have been parsed already. This includes the year, month, day, hour, minute and second values, but also the day-of-week value. Negative relative weekdays are special to the parser and will always map to the weekdays of previous weeks. Because ago is processed while parsing, the meaning of 1 week ago tuesday and 1 week tuesday ago are *not* the same. In the first phrase only the 1 week would be negated, where as in the second phrase *both* 1 week and tuesday are negated. Because ago negates everything that has been parsed, the following phrases are equivalent: 1 week ago, -1 week, 7 days ago and -7 days. This is also true for the following phrases: 1 week ago 2 days, 5 days ago and -5 days (the "2 days" in 1 week ago 2 days is *added* to the -7 days that 1 week ago created as the 2 days itself is not negated.) ago *can* be used multiple times, but then you might get unexpected results. For example 1 week ago 2 days ago actually means +5 days, because the parser does the following steps:

- 1 week creates "7 days"

- ago negates this to "-7 days"

- 2 days makes this "-5 days"

- ago negates this to "5 days"

Another set of phrases is special as well; this week, last week and next week trigger yet another behavior of relative weekday resolving—behavior 2. Besides subtracting seven (last week) days or adding seven days (next week) to the relative day count, they all set the relative weekday to monday and behavior 2. Adding a day name to the phrase then moves the date forward to that day. This means that last week monday and last week are equivalent.

To obtain the Monday of the previous week, you can use Monday ago. The diagram in Figure 6.1 at the end of this chapter shows all these complex behaviors a bit better.

Next Month and Last Month

The next month, last month and similar modifiers that deal with the month might sometimes give unexpected results, take for example, the following code.

```php
<?php
echo date( 'F', strtotime( "2008-01-31 next month" ) ), "\n";
?>
```

This script when run produces the output March, although you would most likely expect it to show February. The unexpected result becomes clearer when you dissect what actually happens. The month modifiers only increase or decrease the value of the month itself. This means that 2008-01-31 next month basically translates to 2008-02-31. Because February does not have 31 days, the day value overflows with two[1] and the date turns into 2008-03-02.

A similar thing happens if you use last month. The output of the script in the following script is thus March. 2008-03-31 last month becomes 2008-02-31, which then again turns into 2008-03-02.

```php
<?php
echo date( 'F', strtotime( "2008-03-31 last month" ) ), "\n";
?>
```

There is a method to obtain the correct behavior, by using the first day of or last day of modifiers. They can be used together with a month specification, such as in last day of next month. The example in the following code uses this special modifier.

---

[1] 2008 is a leap year, and thus the February has 29 days instead of the normal 28 days.

```php
<?php
$d = new DateTime( '2008-01-31 last day of next month' );
echo $d->format( 'F jS, Y' ), "\n";

$d = new DateTime( '2008-02-03 first day of 5 months ago' );
echo $d->format( 'F jS, Y' ), "\n";
?>
```

When run, this script returns:

```
February 29th, 2008
September 1st, 2007
```

When one of the keywords is present, the day-of-month is reset before the correction for overflowed days in a month is corrected. This means that 2008-01-31 last day of next month is first converted to 2008-02-31 like normal. The keyword then makes the parser convert this to 2008-03-00, which is then underflow-corrected to 2008-02-29.

Obtaining Every 3rd Tuesday in each Month

With the DatePeriod iterator class it's fairly easy to return a range of DateTime objects with a specified interval between them. We can use this same method to find all the third Tuesdays in a year. In order to do so we need to set up a start date and end date (both DateTime objects) as well as a specialized DateInterval object create with the DateInterval::createFromDateString() factory method. Only intervals created with the DateInterval::createFromDateString() factory method can contain special relative intervals. In this example, we want each iteration to skip to next month's third Tuesday. Because of the next month part, we need to pick a start date just before the start of the period that we want to gather all third Tuesdays for. In this example we are looking for every third Tuesday in 2008, so we pick as start date 2007-12-31. As an end date we will pick 2008-12-31 because the third Tuesday of every month is guaranteed to be before the 31st of a month. For the interval we will pick the relative time string third tuesday of next month. We do not want the start date being returned from the iterator, so we make sure that it doesn't appear by using the EXCLUDE_START_DATE option when creating the DatePeriod object. Taking all of those parts together, we end up with the example in the following code.

```php
<?php
$db = new DateTime( '2007-12-31' );
$de = new DateTime( '2008-12-31' );
$di = DateInterval::createFromDateString( 'third tuesday of next month' );
$dp = new DatePeriod( $db, $di, $de, DatePeriod::EXCLUDE_START_DATE );

foreach ( $dp as $dt )
{
  echo $dt->format( "l Y-m-d " );
}
?>
```

When this script is run, it returns:

```
Tuesday 2008-01-15  Tuesday 2008-02-19  Tuesday 2008-03-18
Tuesday 2008-04-15  Tuesday 2008-05-20  Tuesday 2008-06-17
Tuesday 2008-07-15  Tuesday 2008-08-19  Tuesday 2008-09-16
Tuesday 2008-10-21  Tuesday 2008-11-18  Tuesday 2008-12-16
```

In the second example, our goal is to list every last Wednesday of each month, at noon. Just like before we pick our start date as 2007-12-31—but we can not pick the end date in the same way either. The end date for iteration is not **part** of the range. Because the last Wednesday in December 2008 is Wednesday 31st, an end date of 2008-12-31 would exclude this last Wednesday of the year. To work around this we simply add one second to the end date.

We can not use the phrase noon in our example, because noon is not considered a relative time string for PHP—it just is an equivalent for saying 12:00. We can also not use the interval phrase last Wed of next month +12 hours because this would show a Thursday every second iteration. The reason for this is that after the first iteration the value would be Wednesday 2008-01-30 12:00. Applying last Wed of next month to this brings this date to Wednesday 2008-02-27 12:00, and then the +12 hours[2] part of the phrase would turn this into Thursday 2008-02-28 00:00. This is not what we

---

[2]+12 hours however does not necessarily mean to advance 12 hours. It merely adds 12 to the hour field in the date time object. This means that +12 hours takes care of DST changeover times, such as in 2008-10-26 +12 hours.

want, so instead we use the interval phrase last Wed of next month and simply apply the extra twelve hours when displaying the value.

The final script follows.

```php
<?php
$db = new DateTime( '2007-12-31' );
$de = new DateTime( '2008-12-31 00:00:01' );
$di = DateInterval::createFromDateString( 'last Wed of next month' );
$dp = new DatePeriod( $db, $di, $de, DatePeriod::EXCLUDE_START_DATE );

foreach ( $dp as $dt )
{
  echo $dt->modify( "+12 hours" )->format( "l Y-m-d H:i\n" );
}
?>
```

When this script is run, it returns:

```
Wednesday 2008-01-30 12:00    Wednesday 2008-02-27 12:00
Wednesday 2008-03-26 12:00    Wednesday 2008-04-30 12:00
Wednesday 2008-05-28 12:00    Wednesday 2008-06-25 12:00
Wednesday 2008-07-30 12:00    Wednesday 2008-08-27 12:00
Wednesday 2008-09-24 12:00    Wednesday 2008-10-29 12:00
Wednesday 2008-11-26 12:00    Wednesday 2008-12-31 12:00
```

Date						
2008-04-11 - Friday	2 weeks ago		1 week friday ago	-2 week friday		2 week ago friday
2008-04-12 - Saturday	2 weeks ago 1 day		1 week saturday ago	-2 week saturday		2 week ago saturday
2008-04-13 - Sunday	2 weeks ago 2 days		1 week sunday ago	-2 week sunday		2 week ago sunday
2008-04-14 - Monday		last week monday	monday ago	-2 week monday		2 week ago monday
2008-04-15 - Tuesday	1 week 3 days ago	last week tuesday	tuesday ago	-2 week tuesday		2 week ago tuesday
2008-04-16 - Wednesday	1 week 2 days ago	last week wednesday	wednesday ago	-2 week wednesday		2 week ago wednesday
2008-04-17 - Thursday	1 week 1 day ago	last week thursday	thursday ago	-2 week thursday		2 week ago thursday
2008-04-18 - Friday	1 week ago	last week friday	friday ago	-1 week friday	last friday	1 week ago friday
2008-04-19 - Saturday	6 days ago	last week saturday	saturday ago	-1 week saturday	last saturday	1 week ago saturday
2008-04-20 - Sunday	5 days ago	last week sunday	sunday ago	-1 week sunday	last sunday	1 week ago sunday
2008-04-21 - Monday	4 days ago	this week monday	-1 week monday ago	-1 week monday	last monday	1 week ago monday
2008-04-22 - Tuesday	3 days ago	this week tuesday	-1 week tuesday ago	-1 week tuesday	last tuesday	1 week ago tuesday
2008-04-23 - Wednesday	2 days ago	this week wednesday	-1 week wednesday ago	-1 week wednesday	last wednesday	1 week ago wednesday
2008-04-24 - Thursday	yesterday	this week thursday	-1 week thursday ago	-1 week thursday	last thursday	1 week ago thursday
2008-04-25 - Friday	today	this week friday	-1 week friday ago	friday		
2008-04-26 - Saturday	tomorrow	this week saturday	-1 week saturday ago	saturday	next saturday	first saturday
2008-04-27 - Sunday	2 days	this week sunday	-1 week sunday ago	sunday	next sunday	first sunday
2008-04-28 - Monday	3 days	next week monday	-2 week monday ago	monday	next monday	first monday
2008-04-29 - Tuesday	4 days	next week tuesday	-2 week tuesday ago	tuesday	next tuesday	first tuesday
2008-04-30 - Wednesday	last day of this month	next week wednesday	-2 week wednesday ago	wednesday	next wednesday	first friday
2008-05-01 - Thursday	first day of next month	next week thursday	-2 week thursday ago	thursday	next thursday	first sunday
2008-05-02 - Friday	1 week	next week friday	-2 week friday ago	+1 week friday	next friday	first friday
2008-05-03 - Saturday	1 week 1 day	next week saturday	-2 week saturday ago	+1 week saturday		second saturday
2008-05-04 - Sunday		next week sunday	-2 week sunday ago	+1 week sunday		second sunday
2008-05-05 - Monday				+1 week monday		second monday
2008-05-06 - Tuesday				+1 week tuesday		second tuesday
2008-05-07 - Wednesday				+1 week wednesday		second wednesday
2008-05-08 - Thursday				+1 week thursday		second thursday
2008-05-09 - Friday	2 week			+2 week friday		second friday

Figure 6.1

Appendix A — Upgrading the Timezone Database

This appendix describes on how to update the timezone database that is bundled with PHP.

Windows

Windows users can download the database from `http://pecl4win.php.net/ext.php/php_timezonedb.dll`[3]

Unix

On Unix-like systems (Linux, Mac OS X, FreeBSD etc.), the database can be installed from sources. There are two ways of doing so. The first one is by using PECL with the command:

```
pecl install timezonedb
```

---

[3]At the moment, the PECL4Win builds are no longer automatically updated. In the future there will be a new build host that will provide updated versions of the timezone database. This means that you can now only use the latest available timezone database through the Windows snapshots, which are available at `http://windows.php.net/snapshots/` and enable the extension in `php.ini` with `extension=php_timezonedb.dll` and restarting the Web server, after placing it in the correct directory. `phpinfo()` shows the directory where to place this downloaded DLL under the `extension_dir` entry.

The second method is by downloading the sources yourself from `http://pecl.php.net/package/timezonedb` and then run the following commands:

```
tar -xvzf timezonedb-*.tgz
cd timezonedb-*
phpize
./configure
make
make install
```

Both methods will compile and install the database, but you still need to add the `extension=timezonedb.so` line in `php.ini`. Both methods also require that you have a correctly set-up PHP installation, including all headers.

Linux users can often find the timezonedb PECL extension in one of the distribution's packages. For example Debian has a package called `php5-timezonedb` which can be installed with:

```
apt-get install php5-timezonedb
```

Gentoo users have an e-build available for the `timezonedb` extension under the name of `dev-php5/pecl-timezonedb`—which at the time of writing still seems to be marked as unstable.

Some distributions, such as RedHat, SUSE, Debian and Ubuntu patch their PHP in such a way that updating the timezone database as mentioned above will not work. These distributions insist on using the system provided timezone database that is available on the file system. This patch makes using timezones much slower on those systems. From PHP 5.3 the format that PHP uses will differ from the system provided timezone database, which makes this patch obsolete. If you're using one of the above mentioned distributions, you will be better off with compiling PHP yourself.

Appendix B — Format Specifiers

date(), DateTime->format(), idate() and strftime() format specifiers

This table lists all the format specifiers for the date(), DateTime->format(), idate() and strftime() functions. For date(), DateTime->format() and idate() those specifiers do not require a prefix; for strftime() the prefix % is required. strftime() specifiers are implemented by the Operating System that PHP is running on, and might not always be available or behave like the table below suggests.

Day

date()	idate()	strftime()	Description	Example
j	d	e	Day of month, numeric	3, 15
d		d	Day of month, 2 digits, leading zero	07, 11
z	z		Day of year, numeric, 0-based	0 (Jan 1st) to 364 or 365 (364 for normal years, 365 for leap years)
		j	Day of year, numeric, 1-based	1 (Jan 1st) to 365 or 366
S			English ordinal day suffix	st, nd, rd

w	w	w	Weekday, numeric, American	0 (Sunday) to 6 (Saturday)
N		u	Weekday, numeric, ISO 8601	1 (Monday) to 7 (Sunday)
D		a	Weekday, textual, three letters	Sun, Mon, Thu
l		A	Weekday, textual, full version	Sunday, Wednesday

Week

date()	idate()	strftime()	Description	Example
W	W	V	Week number, ISO 8601	1, 34, 53
		U	Week number, with Sunday as first day of the week	4, 41
		W	Week number, with Monday as first day of the week	8, 42

Month

date()	idate()	strftime()	Description	Example
n	m		Month, numeric	5, 10
m		m	Month, 2 digits, leading zero	04, 12
M		b	Month, textual, three letters	Feb, Nov
F		B	Month, textual, full version	January, October

t	t		Number of days in month, numeric	1, 28, 31

Year

date()	idate()	strftime()	Description	Example
L	L		Leap year or not	0, 1
		g	Year, 2 digits, ISO 8601	97, 08
o		G	Year, 4 digits, ISO 8601	1997, 2008
y	y	y	Year, 2 digits, natural	96, 08
Y	Y	Y	Year, 4 digits, natural	1996, 2009
		C	Century, 2 digits, leading zero	19, 20

Time

date()	idate()	strftime()	Description	Example
g	h		Hour, 12 hour notation, numeric	1, 6, 12
h		I	Hour, 12 hour notation, leading zero	01, 06, 11
G	H		Hour, 24 hour notation, numeric	0, 7, 14, 23
H		H	Hour, 24 hour notation, leading zero	04, 08, 23
	i		Minutes, numeric	0, 27, 43
i		M	Minutes, leading zero	00, 31, 59
	s		Seconds, numeric	5, 19, 51
s		S	Seconds, leading zero	05, 19, 51

u			Milliseconds, 6 digits, leading zero (Only available when date/- time strings are parsed through new DateTime() and date_create().)	000000, 712312
a		p	am or pm, lower case	am, pm
A			AM or PM, upper case	AM, PM

Timezone

date()	idate()	strftime()	Description	Example
O		z (On some operating systems (such as Windows) the z specifier actually provides a name for the time-zone.)	UTC offset, textual, in hours	-0700, +0200, +0430
P			UTC offset, textual, in hours with colon	-07:00, +10:00
Z	Z		UTC offset, numeric, in seconds	-28800, 3600, 14400

e			Timezone identifier (In case the DateTime object has been created with non-timezone-identifier information, it can also return an timezone abbreviation (T format) or a UTC offset (P format).)	Europe/Oslo, America/Chicago
T		Z	Timezone abbreviation	PDT, GMT, CEST
I	I		Daylight savings time or not	0 or 1

Compound

date()	idate()	strftime()	Description	Example
B	B		Swatch time, 3 digits, leading zero	000, 713, 999
c			ISO 8601 date	2008-05-11T 19:31:07+02:00
r			RFC 2822 date	Sun, 11 May 2008, 19:31:37 +0200
U	U		Seconds since Unix epoch	1210527131
		T	Time, same as %H:%M:%S	21:21:21
		r	Time in am/pm notation	09:16:06 PM
		R	Time in 24 hour notation	21:16:06
		D	Date, American	05/11/08

	c	Preferred date and time format according to locale	locale specific	
	x	Preferred date format according to locale	locale specific	
	X	Preferred time format according to locale	locale specific	

DateTime::createFromFormat(), date_create_from_format() and date_parse_from_format() format specifiers

This table lists all the format specifiers for the `DateInterval->format()` method. There is no prefix required.

Modifier	Description	Example
d j	two digit day with optional leading zero	31, 07
D l	three letter day, or full day name (ignored)	Tuesday, wed
S	English suffix (ignored)	st, nd, rd
z	day of year (0-based, resets month)	43, 081
m n	two digit month with optional leading zero	08

M F	three letter month, or full month name (English)	Mar, December
y	two digit year (0-69 map to 2000-2069, 70-99 map to 1970-1999)	78, 08
Y	four digit year	1978, 2008
g h	two digit hour with optional leading zero (12-hour notation)	04, 11
G H	two digit hour with optional leading zero (24-hour notation)	08, 18
a A	meridian (only when an hour has been parsed	am, p.m. A.M.
i	two digit minute with optional leading zero	06, 53
s	two digit second with optional leading zero	06, 53
u	five digit milliseconds	51231
' '	whitespace (space and tab)	
U	seconds since Unix epoch (always in UTC)	1206115623
e P O T	timezone	Europe/Amsterdam, -04:00, CEST
; : / - . ,	one separation symbol	
\#	any of the above separation symbols	
!	reset all fields to 1970-01-01 00:00:00 in the default timezone	
|	reset all fields to default when not set	
$*$	any sequence of bytes until the next whitespace, separator or digit	
?	any byte & @, (,)	

DateInterval->format() format specifiers

The table on the following page lists all the format specifiers for the `DateInterval->format()` method. Please note that the prefix % is required in order for the format specifiers to work correctly.

Format	Description	Example
Y	Years, numeric, at least 2 digits with leading 0	01, 03
y	Years, numeric	1, 3
M	Months, numeric, at least 2 digits with leading 0	01, 03, 12
m	Months, numeric	1, 3, 12
D	Days, numeric, at least 2 digits with leading 0	01, 03, 31
D	Days, numeric	1, 3, 31
a	Total amount of days	4, 18, 8123
H	Hours, numeric, at least 2 digits with leading 0	01, 03, 23
h	Hours, numeric	1, 3, 23
I	Minutes, numeric, at least 2 digits with leading 0	01, 03, 59
i	Minutes, numeric	1, 3, 59
S	Seconds, numeric, at least 2 digits with leading 0	01, 03, 57
s	Seconds, numeric	1, 3, 57
R	Sign: - when negative, + when positive	-, +
r	Sign: - when negative, empty when positive	-,
%	Literal: %	%

Appendix C — Parser Formats

This appendix describes all the different formats that the strtotime(), new DateTime() and date_create() parser understands. The formats are grouped by section. In most cases formats from different sections can be used in the same date/-time string. For each of the supported formats, one or more examples are given, as well as a description for the format. Characters in single quotes in the formats are case-insensitive ('t' could be t or T), characters in double quotes are case-sensitive ("T" is only T).

Time Formats

Used Symbols

Description	Format	Examples
frac	. [0-9]+	".21342", ".85"
hh	"0"?[1-9] | "1"[0-2]	"04", "7", "12"
HH	[01][0-9] | "2"[0-4]	"04", "7", "19"
meridian	[AaPp] .? [Mm] .? \ 0 \ t]	"A.m.", "pM", "am."
MM	[0-5][0-9]	"00", "12", "59"
II	[0-5][0-9]	"00", "12", "59"
space	[\ t]+	

| tz | "("? [A-Za-z]{1,6} ")"? \| [A-Z][a-z]+([_/][A-Z][a-z]+)+; | "CEST", "Europe/Amsterdam", "America/Indiana/-Knox" |
| tzcorrection | "GMT"? [+-] hh ":"? MM ? | "+0400", "GMT-07:00", "-07:00" |

12 Hour Notation

Description	Format	Examples
Hour only, with meridian	hh *space*? meridian	"4 am", "5PM"
Hour and minutes, with meridian	hh [.:] MM *space*? meridian	"4:08 am", "7:19P.M."
Hour, mins and seconds, with meridian	hh [.:] MM [.:] II *space*? meridian	"4:08:37 am", "7:19:19P.M."
MS SQL (Hour, minutes, seconds and fraction with meridian) (PHP 5.3 and later only)	hh ":" MM ":" II [.:] [0-9]+ meridian	"4:08:39:12313am"

24 Hour Notation

Description	Format	Examples
Hour and minutes	't'? HH [.:] MM	"04:08", "19.19", "T23:43"
Hour and minutes, no colon	't'? HH MM	"0408", "t1919", "T2343"
Hour, minutes and seconds	't'? HH [.:] MM [.:] II	"04.08.37", "t19:19:19"
Hour, minutes and seconds, no colon	't'? HH MM II	"040837", "T191919"
Hour, minutes, seconds and timezone	't'? HH [.:] MM [.:] II *space*? (tzcorrection | tz)	"040837CEST", "T191919-0700"
Hour, minutes, seconds and fraction	't'? HH [.:] MM [.:] II frac	"04.08.37.81412", "19:19:19.532453"
Time zone information	tz | tzcorrection	"CEST", "Europe/Amsterdam", "+0430", "GMT-06:00"

Date Formats

Used Symbols

Description	Format	Examples
daysuf	"st" | "nd" | "rd" | "th"	
dd	([0-2]?[0-9] | "3"[01]) daysuf?	"7th", "22nd", "31"
DD	"0" [0-9] | [1-2][0-9] | "3" [01]	"07", "31"
m	'january' | 'february' | 'march' | 'april' | 'may' | 'june' | 'july' | 'august' | 'september' | 'october' | 'november' | 'december' | 'jan' | 'feb' | 'mar' | 'apr' | 'may' | 'jun' | 'jul' | 'aug' | 'sep' | 'sept' | 'oct' | 'nov' | 'dec' | "I" | "II" | "III" | "IV" | "V" | "VI" | "VII" | "VIII" | "IX" | "X" | "XI" | "XII"	
M	'jan' | 'feb' | 'mar' | 'apr' | 'may' | 'jun' | 'jul' | 'aug' | 'sep' | 'sept' | 'oct' | 'nov' | 'dec'	
mm	"0"? [0-9] | "1"[0-2]	"0", "04", "7", "12"
MM	"0" [0-9] | "1"[0-2]	"00", "04", "07", "12"
y	[0-9]\1,4\	"00", "78", "08", "8", "2008"
yy	[0-9]\2\	"00", "08", "78"
YY	[0-9]\4\	"2000", "2008", "1978"

Localized Notations

Description	Format	Examples
American month and day	mm "/" dd	"5/12", "10/27"

American month, day and year	mm "/" dd "/" y	"12/22/78", "1/17/2006", "1/17/6"
Four digit year, month and day with slashes	YY "/" mm "/" dd	"2008/6/30", "1978/12/22"
Four digit year and month (GNU)	YY "-" mm	"2008-6", "2008-06", "1978-12"
Year, month and day with dashes	y "-" mm "-" dd	"2008-6-30", "78-12-22", "8-6-21"
Day, month and four digit year, with dots, tabs or dashes	dd [.\ t-] mm [.-] YY	"30-6-2008", "22.12\ t1978"
Day, month and two digit year, with dots or tabs	dd [.\ t] mm "." yy	"30.6.08", "22\ t12\ t78"
Day, textual month and year	dd ([\ t.-])* m ([\ t.-])* y	"30-June 2008", "22DEC78", "14 III 1879"
Textual month and four digit year (Day reset to 1)	m ([\ t.-])* YY	"June 2008", "DEC1978", "March 1879"

Four digit year and textual month (Day reset to 1)	YY ([\ t.-])* m	"2008 June", "1978-XII", "1879.MARCH"
Textual month, day and year	m ([.\ t-])* dd [,.stndrh\ t]+ y	"July 1st, 2008", "April 17, 1790", "May.9,78"
Textual month and day	m ([.\ t-])* dd [,.stndrh\ t]*	"July 1st,", "Apr 17", "May.9"
Day and textual month	d ([.\ t-])* m	"1 July", "17 Apr", "9.May"
Month abbreviation, day and year	M "-" DD "-" y	"May-09-78", "Apr-17-1790"
Year, month abbreviation and day	y "-" M "-" DD	"78-Dec-22", "1814-MAY-17"
Year (and just the year)	YY	"1978", "2008"
Textual month (and just the month)	m	"March", "jun", "DEC"

ISO8601 Notations

Description	Format	Examples
Eight digit year, month and day	YY MM DD	"15810726", "19780417", "18140517"
Four digit year, month and day with slashes	YY "/" MM "/" DD	"2008/06/30", "1978/12/22"
Two digit year, month and day with dashes	yy "-" MM "-" DD	"08-06-30", "78-12-22"
Four digit year with optional sign, month and day	[+-]? YY "-" MM "-" DD	"-0002-07-26", "+1978-04-17", "1814-05-17"

The following should be noted:

For the y and yy formats, years below 100 are handled in a special way when the y or yy symbol is used. If the year falls in the range 0 inclusive) to 69 (inclusive), 2000 is added. If the year falls in the range 70 (inclusive) to 99 (inclusive) then 1900 is added. This means that 00-01-01 is interpreted as 2000-01-01.

The "Day, month and two digit year, with dots or tabs" format (dd [.\ t] mm "." yy) only works for the year values 61 (inclusive) to 99 (inclusive). Outside those years the time format HH [.:] MM [.:] SS has precedence.

The "Year (and just the year)" format only works if a time string has already been found. Otherwise this format is recognised as HH MM.

It is possible to over- and underflow the dd and DD format. Day 0 means the last day of previous month, whereas overflows count into the next month. This makes 2008-08-00 equivalent to 2008-07-31 and 2008-06-31 equivalent to 2008-07-01 (June only has 30 days).

It is also possible to underflow the mm and MM formats with the value 0. A month value of 0 means December of the previous year. As example 2008-00-22 is equivalent to 2007-12-22.

If you combine the previous two facts and underflow both the day and the month, the following happens: 2008-00-00 first gets converted to 2007-12-00 which then gets converted to 2007-11-30. This also happens with the string 0000-00-00, which gets transformed into -0001-11-30 (the year -1 in the ISO 8601 calendar, which is 2 BC in the proleptic Gregorian calendar).

Compound Formats

Used Symbols

Description	Format	Examples
DD	"0" [0-9] | [1-2][0-9] | "3" [01]	"02", "12", "31"
doy	"00"[1-9] | "0"[1-9][0-9] | [1-2][0-9][0-9] | "3"[0-5][0-9] | "36"[0-6]	"000", "012", "366"
frac	. [0-9]+	".21342", ".85"
hh	[01]?[0-9] | "2"[0-4]	"1", "7", "08", "23"
HH	[01][0-9] | "2"[0-4]	"01", "07", "23"
ii	[0-5][0-9]	"04", "8", "59"
II	[0-5][0-9]	"04", "08", "59"
M	'jan' | 'feb' | 'mar' | 'apr' | 'may' | 'jun' | 'jul' | 'aug' | 'sep' | 'sept' | 'oct' | 'nov' | 'dec'	
MM	"0" [0-9] | "1" [0-2]	"02", "12"
space	[\ t]+	
ss	[0-5][0-9]	"04", "8", "59"
SS	[0-5][0-9]	"04", "08", "59"
W	"0"[1-9] | [1-4][0-9] | "5"[0-3]	"05", "17", "53"
tzcorrection	"GMT"? [+-] HH ":"? II?	"+0400", "GMT-07:00", "-07:00"
YY	[0-9]{4}	"2000", "2008", "1978"

Localized Notations

Description	Format	Examples
Common Log Format	dd "/" M "/" YY : HH ":" II ":" SS *space* tzcorrection	"10/Oct/2000:13:55:36 -0700"
EXIF	YY ":" MM ":" DD " " HH ":" II ":" SS	"2008:08:07 18:11:31"
ISO year with ISO week	YY "-"? "W" W	"2008W27", "2008-W28"
ISO year with ISO week and day	YY "-"? "W" W "-"? [0-7]	"2008W273", "2008-W28-3"
PostgreSQL: Year with day-of-year	YY "."? doy	"2008.197", "2008197"
SOAP	YY "-" MM "-" DD "T" HH ":" II ":" SS frac tzcorrection?	"2008-07-01T22:35:17.02", "2008-07-01T22:35:17.03+08:00"
Unix Timestamp	"@" "-"? [0-9]+	"@1215282385"
XMLRPC	YY MM DD "T" hh ":" II ":" SS	"20080701T22:38:07", "20080701T9:38:07"
XMLRPC (Compact)	YY MM dd 't' hh II SS	"20080701t223807", "20080701T093807"
WDDX	YY "-" mm "-" dd "T" hh ":" ii ":" ss	"2008-7-1T9:3:37"

The following should be noted:

The "W" in the "ISO year with ISO week" and "ISO year with ISO week and day" formats is case-sensitive; you can only use the upper case "W".

The "T" in the "SOAP", "XMRPC" and "WDDX" formats is case-sensitive; you can only use the upper case "T".

For a more thorough description of *relative time*, please see Chapter 5—"Date/-Time Manipulation."

Relative Formats

Used Symbols

Description	Format	Examples
dayname	'sunday' | 'monday' | 'tuesday' | 'wednesday' | 'thursday' | 'friday' | 'saturday' | 'sun' | 'mon' | 'tue' | 'wed' | 'thu' | 'fri' | 'sat' | 'sun'	
daytext	*dayname* | 'weekday' | 'weekdays'	
number	[+-]?[0-9]+	
ordinal	'first' | 'second' | 'third' | 'fourth' | 'fifth' | 'sixth' | 'seventh' | 'eight' | 'ninth' | 'tenth' | 'eleventh' | 'twelfth' | 'next' | 'last' | 'previous' | 'this'	
reltext	'next' | 'last' | 'previous' | 'this'	
space	[\ t]+	
unit	(('sec' | 'second' | 'min' | 'minute' | 'hour' | 'day' | 'fortnight' | 'forthnight' | 'month' | 'year') 's'?) | 'weeks' | *daytext*	

Day-based Notations

Description	Format	Examples
'yesterday'	Midnight of yesterday	"yesterday 14:00"
'midnight'	The time is set to 00:00:00	
'today'	The time is set to 00:00:00	
'now'	Now --- this is simply ignored	
'noon'	The time is set to 12:00:00	"yesterday noon"
'tomorrow'	Midnight of tomorrow	

'back of' *hour* (PHP 5.3 and later only)	15 minutes past the specified hour	"back of 7pm", "back of 15"
'front of' *hour* (PHP 5.3 and later only)	15 minutes before the specified hour	"front of 5am", "front of 23"
'first day' ' of'? (PHP 5.3 and later only)	Sets the day of the first of the current month. This phrase is best used together with a month name following it.	"first day of January 2008"
'last day' ' of'? (PHP 5.3 and later only)	Sets the day to the last day of the current month. This phrase is best used together with a month name following it.	"last day of next month"
ordinal *space* dayname *space* 'of' (PHP 5.3 and later only)	Calculates the x-th week day of the current month.	"first sat of July 2008"
'last' *space* dayname *space* 'of' (PHP 5.3 and later only)	Calculates the "last" week day of the current month.	"last sat of July 2008"
number space? (unit | 'week')	Handles relative time items where the value is a number.	"+5 weeks", "12 day", "-7 weekdays"
ordinal *space* unit	Handles relative time items where the value is text.	"fifth day", "second month"

'ago'	Negates all the values of previously found relative time items.	"2 days ago", "8 days ago 14:00", "2 months 5 days ago", "2 months ago 5 days", "2 days ago ago"
dayname	Moves to the next day of this name; Chapter 6 has an in-depth explanation.	"Monday"
reltext *space* 'week'	Handles the special format "weekday + last/this/next week".	"Monday next week"

Important is to note the few different behaviors regarding relative weekdays.

Relative statements are always processed *after* non-relative statements. This makes +1 week july 2008 and july 2008 +1 week equivalent. yesterday, midnight, today, noon and tomorrow are an exception to this rule. tomorrow 11:00 and 11:00 tomorrow are different. Considering today's date of July 23rd, 2008 the first one produces 2008-07-24 11:00 where as the second one produces 2008-07-24 00:00. The reason for this is is that those six statements directly influence the current time.

Please also observe the following remarks when the current day-of-week is the same as the day-of-week used in the date/time string. The current day-of-week could have been (re-)calculated by non-relative parts of the date/time string however.

- dayname—does *not* advance to another day. (Example: Wed July 23rd, 2008 means 2008-07-23).

- *number* dayname—does *not* advance to another day. (Example: 1 wednesday july 23rd, 2008 means 2008-07-23).

- *number* week dayname—will first add the number of weeks, but does *not* advance to another day. In this case *number* week and dayname are two distinct blocks. (Example: +1 week wednesday july 23rd, 2008 means 2008-07-30).

- ordinal dayname—*does* advance to another day. (Example first wednesday july 23rd, 2008 means 2008-07-30).

- *number* week ordinal dayname—will first add the number of weeks, and then *advances* to another day. In this case *number* week and ordinal dayname are two distinct blocks. (Example: `+1 week first wednesday july 23rd, 2008` means `2008-08-06`).

- `ordinal dayname 'of'` —does *not* advance to another day. (Example: `first wednesday of july 23rd, 2008` means `2008-07-02` because the specific phrase with 'of' resets the day-of-month to '1' and the '23rd' is ignored here).

Also observe that the `of` in ordinal *space* dayname *space* 'of' and last *space* dayname *space* 'of' does something special.

- It sets the day-of-month to 1.

- `ordinal dayname 'of'` —does *not* advance to another day. (Example: `first tuesday of july 2008` means `2008-07-01`).

- `ordinal dayname` —*does* advance to another day. (Example: `first tuesday july 2008` means `2008-07-08`—see also point 4 in the list above).

- `'last' dayname 'of'` —takes the last dayname of the current month. (Example: `last wed of july 2008` means `2008-07-30`)

- `'last' dayname`—takes the last dayname from the current day. (Example: `last wed july 2008` means `2008-06-25`. `july 2008` first sets the current date to `2008-07-01` and then `last wed` moves to the previous Wednesday which is `2008-06-25`.

Index

www.ingramcontent.com/pod-product-compliance
Lightning Source LLC
Chambersburg PA
CBHW080420060326
40689CB00019B/4319